How Can We Find True Love

The 12 Steps to Spirituality

A Christian View of
Spiritual Growth
Through the Process
of the 12 Step Program

Written by: Bill J.

For information please contact: Vision Management
                                   5202 Fox Trail Lane
                                   Colleyville, Texas 76034
                                   817-355-1816

Winepress Publishing
MUKILTEO, WA 98275

Book Dedication

The gift of my life began with the Lord and to God be all praise and love.

It began with two special people whose love and dedication to God's will gave me life. To these two, who have shared and helped me find my way, I dedicate this work. Mom & Dad, you have blessed me and shown me the true way to my Savior's house. For this wonderful gift of love, I thank you.

To those who have been part of my journey, especially my wife, I also bow in grateful honor. Without each and every one of you these words would never have been put on paper. My peace and friendship are yours forever.

Permission from A.A. World Services for Adaptation of the Twelve Steps

1. We admitted we were powerless over alcohol - that our lives had become unmanageable. 2. Came to believe that a Power greater than ourselves could restore us to sanity. 3. Made a decision to turn our will and our lives over to the care of God as we understood Him. 4. Made a searching and fearless moral inventory of ourselves. 5. Admitted to God, to ourselves and to another human being the exact nature of our wrongs. 6. Were entirely ready to have God remove all these defects of character. 7. Humbly asked Him to remove our shortcomings. 8. Made a list of all persons we had harmed, and became willing to make amends to them all. 9. Made direct amends to such people wherever possible, except when to do so would injure them or others. 10. Continued to take personal inventory and when we were wrong promptly admitted it. 11. Sought through prayer and meditation to improve our conscious contact with God *as we understood Him*, praying only for the knowledge of His will and the power to carry that out. 12. Having had a spiritual awakening as a result of these Steps, we tried to carry this message to alcoholics, and to practice these principles in all our affairs.

Table of Contents

Introduction

Dear Friend:

I send you this to share my joy and love for the 12 Step Program and hope you find it valuable in your personal journey with Christ.

Beginnings

I write out of a need to grow and understand the love I have received from Our Creator through Jesus Christ. This, above all, needs to be acknowledged and proclaimed. My joy and my longings all belong to Christ, my special friend, and the One who has led me to God's infinite love.

For each writer, there is an urgency to get a message out. It is my prayer that the urging comes from the grace of Jesus and that the message has not been tainted by my slow and stumbling growth. It has been this growth, through the 12 Steps, and the inner peace and knowledge that makes me write. I have seen and felt the workings of Our Savior in my life and seen the wonderful miracle of His saving power in others I have sponsored on this 12 Step journey. Now I invite you to partake in the wonderful grace of Our Creator through the saving message of Jesus Christ.

It is the Steps that gave me the direction and the logical progression of emotion, feeling, and knowledge so that

I could find my way into the loving arms of Christ. This is how I found Him. This is how I must share the message He has given to me.

May this message of love and service bring us closer to our Lord and fill us with the joy of His kingdom here on earth.

Outline of This Book

I have separated each chapter into three major topics:
      Preparation
      Personal Goals
      Discipline
Each of these provides a structure and formatted body of information so that the book can be used effectively. The following is a short description of each section.

Preparation

This section will set down the basic tasks, activities and methods for getting ready to work the particular step. It will provide the elements of our work and the basic gifts to be gained from this part of the journey.

Setting Your Personal Goals

Our short term goals can be seen as daily requirements for working on the particular step we are on. As such, they need to be understood, mastered and made part of the basic process we will work into our lives.

Our long term goals will look to the continuation of each step "as part of our new Christian lives." As such, they will take more time and even more discipline to master. However, each long term goal will be centered around the basic principle of the step and will fit within the pattern of grace and discipleship found on this journey with Jesus Christ.

Discipline

Unlike many "self-help" books, we will not find a soft-soap message. This thing called Christianity is a process of becoming more pleasing to Our Lord and Savior. As disciples, we take up the cross Christ gives to us and follow a path very few choose to travel. The 12 Step Program also presents a path less traveled and while it invites us to join, it never disputes that it is through discipline and perseverance that the gifts of the program are gained.

This section presents my understanding of the actions we must take to make these steps part of our lives and therefore find our way to the Love of Christ.

Personal Remarks

My journey has given me more joy and more fulfillment than anything I could have ever dreamed. The promises of the 12 Step Program have been fulfilled and I have only just begun.

There are many programs and paths to Our Creator. The one sure path is through Jesus Christ. I believe this 12 Step Program is indeed a direct and logical path to Christ and therefore to God.

You may find that you do not need this discipline, and that is OK. You may not be able to take the steps and disciplines necessary to follow this program of love and service, and that is still OK. Jesus loves each and every one of us and will find a way to bring us home. I hope that you too will experience Christ's love for you.

I Have a Vision

I have a vision that I will walk hand in hand with Jesus. So tender and loving is this dream that I know it comes from deep within my soul and is filled with the spirit of our loving shepherd.

This vision will see the fellowship of Christ join in true peace and love to share and enjoy the kingdom of Christ's community here today.

I asked once, in the darkness of my life, where He was? Why I could not feel Him. Why I hurt so much? This was what He said to me:

On a retreat weekend in October of 1983, I met a man who would change my life forever. Mike McK., in order to explain how faith worked within his life, shared his pain and trials with alcohol. In this stirring statement he professed his life long need for Christ to be his Higher Power. Without Christ he would have died alone and in disease.

There in a few moments of a weekend retreat I felt the power of God. There for a fleeting moment I truly understood what others had preached about for so long. God is love and God loves me. I soared from this weekend ready, willing, but not able to change my whole life. It was not my time and, inexorably, I failed again and again to capture the emotional moment of that weekend.

For me the problem would continue for another nine months. (I was giving birth to a new me!) I would attempt to be the new god rather than finding the way to be in His service and therefore find the true peace He wanted for me all along. It was at the height of this suffering, (being so close to Christ and not finding Him is the worst form of pain I know), that I reached out and called on the man Christ sent me months before. You see I was also troubled by the same disease as Mike and I needed special help. It was only through those chosen by God to minister in this special way that I could truly find my way home.

And so, July 4 1984, I entered a 12 Step program and began a journey that would bring me to Christ. A simple process of moving from self-centered to God-centered. A logical progression of baby steps taken to find what I had missed all of my life. July 4th 1984 was the first day of my new life and I had found peace.

I have a vision that I will walk hand in hand with Jesus.

I asked again why I found Him here? This is what He said to me:

For each of us there is a way to the Creator. For all of us this way is through Jesus Christ. In seeing the special needs of His children, no matter what the aliment or disorder, He sends those who can bring His children to the Lord in a special way.

The 12 Step Program of recovery was God's special gift given through the loving and caring hands of servants sent to do the Lord's work.

I have a vision that I will walk hand in hand with Jesus.

I asked again what did He want me to do? This is what He said to me:

This wonderful gift of love through the 12 Steps has filled my life and given me the way to the Lord. Christianity is now alive and real to me and my life is finally whole. Christ's kingdom is all of the world and filled with all of His precious children. He gave me this way so I could pass it on in joy and love and service. He gave me this way so I can have joy in Him!

I have a vision and I want to share this vision with you. It is a vision of a carpenter's son from long ago who came into our lives and showed us the true and everlasting love of Our Creator in heaven. I walked an interesting pathway with some friends of His and they showed me that His kingdom is truly here today, and each of us can share in His love and tender kindness.

I hope you will join with me and share this vision of love and service.

THE 12 STEP PROGRAM

The next pages contain the path of the 12 Steps to Recovery on a spiritual level for Christians. Many others may find both joy and peace in these words, accepting these words with open hearts and minds, to reflect on their own spiritual growth with their particular "Higher Power." I, myself, can only write the message that I know to be truth.

The Miracle of the 12 Step Program

The program of Alcoholics Anonymous is and will continue to be a very special gift from God. Spiritually inspired, it has drawn from the knowledge of the world, the scriptures, and man's intimacy with God to provide hope and encouragement for those who have lost their way.

The history as related in "Alcoholics Anonymous Comes of Age" provides a wonderful view of this miracle in modern times. How a few people inspired and in need found the keys to the very kingdom of heaven here on earth.

Before all else, one must see and understand the history that goes behind the movement. **"Investigation prior to judgement"** is vital to fully understanding the impact and inspiration of this movement. Given the time and the willingness, you will see where and how Christ has touched the world through this program. And, more important to our personal journey, how this program and its principles fit and fulfill our spiritual needs.

All references to the 12 Steps of Alcoholics Anonymous and use of the steps for this program are with prior written consent of AA World Services, Inc. and do not reflect their agreement with any portion of this Spiritual Program. My respect and undying gratitude for this organization will remain vivid in my daily joy.

The Anonymity Concept

Bill W. and Dr. Bob struggled with ego and a critical need for money to expand and "sell" their new found freedom from alcohol. But time and again they ran into one significant obstacle:

What if we fail? How will others perceive our failure? How will it effect the program?

And so, almost reluctantly, they developed and nurtured the concept of Anonymity. The program traditions state it this way:

Tradition 12: Anonymity is the spiritual foundation of all our traditions, ever reminding us to place principles before personalities.

Tradition 11: Our public relations policy is based on attraction rather than promotion; we need always maintain personal anonymity at the level of press, radio and films.

Fostering such a principle in a Christian Development Work seems a little funny, but let's look a little deeper at the issues and principles involved.

We will change very little of the basic program as inspired and given to Bill W. & Dr. Bob. We will only remove the word "Alcohol" and replace it with "SIN." Other than citing Biblical references, we will change nothing else delivered within the original 12 Step Program. The question is what should be done with Anonymity?

Too many times we humans fail to see the essence of Anonymity. It is not that we cannot proclaim our Lord. It is that we must not put ourselves in the place of the Lord. Seek prayerfully the wonderful humility presented by the founding fathers of this program. Setting themselves aside they allowed our Higher Power to take His rightful place in our recovery and our lives. Maybe a lesson could be learned by some of our "preachers" today.

Anonymity is a spiritual foundation that needs to be included within any witnessing program. I cannot become the center of the program but I can be the vessel of Christ's message. That is more than enough for me and a joyful and fulfilling path for my work in His vineyard.

Take the First Step

Before we begin, let us set the stage for the journey. Many will look within the cover of this book and become a little confused.

✟   Maybe they will not see a disease to use for this program or as we will call it a "DIS-ease."

✟   Maybe they will see this process as a search for something wrong and feel their life is OK the way it is and not choose to look any further.

✟   Maybe they will have followed this 12 Step path before and do not see the need to go over it again.

This is a journey of faith begining with the essence of humanity and leading to the humble honesty of humanity alive in Christ. I have yet to meet the person who would not benefit from this journey. I have yet to reach a point in my own journey where I have learned enough about this program and can put it on a shelf.

I have also never met a person who *NEEDED* this program but did not *WANT IT* that has been successful in the journey. So here is our dilemma and our staring point. Will you go on? Will you give this program a chance?

For those of us who have had a physical or emotional malady it may have been a little easier. We were told to give it a period of time and if it worked continue, if it did not work then move on.

Simple? I give you the same challenge. Take some time from your life and some space within your heart. Set it aside for the process of this journey and join me in the *12 Steps to Spirituality*. If, after reading and reflecting on this program, you see no use for your personal spiritual growth then move on and God's speed. If, however, there is a new yearning, a new hope, and new path opened to you, join us on this happy road to destiny!

This is the beginning. Nothing flashy or mystical. Nothing complex or life altering. All of those changes come from God not the words of this book. The changes you seek will be yours if you are willing to work for them and they will ALL come from your Higher Power, Jesus Christ.

The Joys of the Journey

In the next few pages I will capsulize the promises of the 12 Step program of Alcohol Anonymous as found in the Big Book, the corresponding promises found in the Bible (The Big Big Book). As you reflect on these promises seek to hear and feel the response from your inner soul.

Not too many ages ago a man entered our human existence and changed the world for all time. He, in humility and great peace, opened up a new way of life for those that CHOOSE to follow Him. With arms outstretched, He forgave all sin and allowed us to become one with Him and His Father in Heaven.

Christian Choose!
  "Follow Me," He said.
  "How?" we cried.
With love and service.

The Promises from the AA Big Book

Page 63:
1. As we felt new Power flow in, as we enjoyed peace of mind, as we discovered we could face

life successfully, as we became conscious of His presence, we began to lose our fear of today, tomorrow or the hereafter. We were reborn.

Page 83-84:

1. We will be amazed before we are half way through.
2. We are going to know a new freedom and a new way of life.
3. We will not regret the past nor wish to shut the door on it.
4. We will comprehend the word serenity and we will know peace.
5. No matter how far down the scale we have gone, we will see how our experience can benefit others.
6. That feeling of uselessness and self pity will disappear.
7. We will loose interest in selfish things and gain interest in our fellows.
8. Self-seeking will slip away.
9. Our whole attitude and outlook on life will change.
10. Fear of people and of economic insecurity will leave us.
11. We will intuitively know how to handle situations which used to baffle us.
12. We will suddenly realize that God is doing for us what we could not do for ourselves.

Are these extravagant promises? We think not. They are fulfilled among us - sometimes quickly, sometimes slowly. They will always materialize if we work for them.

Page 100

1.   When we look back, we realize that the things which came to us when we put ourselves in God's hands were better than anything we could have planned.

Page 120

1.   You will loose your old life and find one much better.

The Promises from the BIG BIG Book

1.   Those who give to the poor shall be rewarded (Matthew 6:4)
2.   God hears our prayer and knows our needs (Matthew 6:5-9)
3.   Those who ask, search, and knock on the doors of life for grace will receive it (Matthew 7:7-11)
4.   God will give the Holy Spirit to those who ask (Luke 11:9-13)
5.   Living according to Christ's way will bring stability into life (Matthew 7:27)
6.   Those who follow Christ shall find rest for their souls (Matthew 18:19-20)
7.   Christians shall receive payment many time over in this life for following Jesus (Luke 18:28-30)
8.   Christ will be present when two or more are gathered in His name (Matthew 18:19-20)
9.   Those who believe in Jesus shall do the same works that He did (John 14:12)
10.   Jesus will give to His followers a peace that surpasses understanding (John 14:27)

11. If we remain in Christ, we may ask what we will and we shall get it (John 15:7)
12. Living the Christian life will bring us joy (John 16:24)

The list could go on and on! These are all promises that can be tested, and, in fact, have been confirmed millions of times during the course of Christian history. They apply for the most part to spiritual matters, but is this not the area of life where we need the most encouragement anyway?

Now read again the promises. Can you see His Kingdom of love and service? The light is not at the end of dark tunnels. The light is Christ and He is here with us today.

My reasoning for opening with the promises from the Big Book and the Big Big Book is to set the goal we need in our personal darkness. If we are in pain and cannot feel Christ within our lives; if we are comfortable in our life but still filled with an emptiness we cannot explain; then we may want to choose a new and different path to fill this void. This is the path we will explore together in the 12 Step Process of Spirituality.

Sayings

The Heart of the Child

In looking for a place to begin my own journey I find constant torment from the verse within the bible:

"Amen, I say to you, whoever does not accept the kingdom of God like a child will not enter it" (Mark 10:15, Luke 18:17).

This warning within the scripture is paramount to my full acceptance of God's love. I can find no other way to the Creator except through the heart of a child.

It is truly amazing how worn out and clouded I become when I use the wonderful power of the intellect God has given me to solve the mysteries of the world. I immediately feel as if I must accomplish something. I must reach a goal, or conquer a foe, or create something from nothing. The amazement is not the true and awesome power of my mind for that is a real and an exciting gift from my Creator in heaven. The amazing thing is my immediate jump into "I."

For me the mind or intellect, on its own, will lead to a selfish place of control of the world around me. It just seems to work that way, to be a part of what it is to be human. Of all the theories on original sin, this is the one that fits best the explanation within my soul. The tree of knowledge is just what it implies, a wonderful gift we are unable to handle. Intellect is power that leads us away from Christ and to selfish accomplishments, and yet a true and wonderful gift from Our Creator.

Herein lies my dilemma. How can I use this intellect and still remain in the arms of the carpenter? How can I bring myself into His control while I search the depths of my faith?

I have always sensed the joy in Jesus' heart when He was around children. I can see Him in my mind's eye getting down in the dusty street to romp and play with them when no one was pulling on Him and trying to make Him "perform". I can understand the need He must have felt to be playful and free. And yet my weak and undisciplined consciousness holds me from acceptance of this way of life with Christ. I still want to say, "Sure it is fun to play, but we have work to do and a soul to save. We can't waste our time in childish games."

Over and over a warning fills my mind and reaches somewhere deep inside my soul. *"Do not pass by this message. Do not let yourself be fooled. He did not come here to tell you things you do not need."* Over and over I feel the ancient urge to cry out to the heavens "Come down here and answer me. Show me what you mean!"

It would certainly be a cruel and punishing God who would set us on a journey built around a "Catch 22." To give us the power of intellect and, by its very use, have us loose that which we seek.

No. There is a desire of our Creator to have us learn and understand the Lord. There is a powerful and ever-present urge within the human spirit to reach out into the eternity and touch the Hand of God, to be in relationship with the Creator, and to be one with the Spirit of Love.

Even more so, it would be an awful and vindictive God who expected homage and dull reverence based upon non-use of the intellect. Some certainly have tried this route of "worship" and found ways to lead people astray.

No. There can be no doubt that our very humanity is a gift from God and this includes our intellect. We are indeed expected to use this intellect to seek God and come to the Lord in love and understanding.

How then do I accomplish my journey with the use of this "selfish laden" intellect? How can I remain in the child?

The Tools of a Child

The journey of the 12 Steps will fill in the gaps and provide the needed nourishment for the soul so that our spirit may become one with Christ. This path will take time and patience and perseverance. In the beginning of the journey, therefore, we will use these "Child Tools" to make the way simpler and safer.

What must be done now is not function but attitude. It is not what we learn but how we learn it. Attitude is how we accept the gifts we will receive. We must maintain this attitude throughout the journey. Here is the answer to this warning within the scriptures. Here is where we need to concentrate our daily prayers and focus our day's work.

Those who traveled this pathway before us have touched all the dilemmas we will touch and their wisdom pours out in abundance for our free and grateful use. The founders, seeing those early in the journey troubled by the awesome task, gave us tools to "play with" and to use with reverence and gratefulness throughout our lives. These I call the tools of the Child because they focus us on the message of the scriptures and the joy to be found in solving the parable of the child.

One Day at A Time

Of all the tools, this one must be understood and its value incorporated within the very nature of our being. As spirits able to handle complex and abstract ideas, we can think about the future and imagine the outcome of events. Herein lies the tempting power key. We see an outcome and we feel it is both logical and good. We therefore request and indeed demand that God make it so. Here we allow our "self" to, once again, take over the work of the Lord.

Our childish games of power are the ingrained desire to improve the process as quickly as possible. And yet when all is said and done the workings of God in our lives are much more wonderful than any imaginings we could have produced on our own.

And so the first tool is to live *"One Day at A Time"*. This comes from the wonderful serenity prayer *"...living one day at a time, enjoying one moment at a time...."* which points us in the proper direction intellectually. We ask for three things from God in this serenity prayer. Listen carefully to our request:

> Serenity,
> Courage, and
> Wisdom.

These are not requests of someone who will travel though time and space mindless of or in fear of their humanity. It is a request for the gifts to discern and do what is proper in God's kingdom. It is the request for the proper use of the gift of intelligence.

What *"One Day at A Time"* does for us is take away the areas where the outcome is beyond our efforts. It allows us to focus on the areas in our lives where Christ wants our active and intellectual efforts and assistance. It gives us the power of our minds without the dangers of our selfish nature turning on us.

It is the first tool of the child, and one of the key tools for finding the kingdom of God.

Keep it Simple

To kiss is to allow a nearness and vulnerability that defies the tendencies and fears of our nature. It is interesting that we use this to form an acronym of caution. *"Keep it Simple (and Steady)"* is one of the tools heard very often from sponsors within the 12 Step journey. And from personal experience a statement that is not over-used!

"Keep it Simple" is a tool to focus and rethink one's own actions. It helps us to stand back from our intended actions and make sure where we are going and what we are doing.

I find it helpful to understand that if an event becomes complicated and requires many actions, it probably has a better solution. This is a basic law of any work environment and can normally be accepted by all. This allows us to break down tasks and ideas to their elemental actions so we can comprehend and accomplish them.

This tool uses the same process for controlling our tendencies to stray from the path. I believe it is based upon the experience of the ages which shows no complex theological finding has improved the simple path of faith and love. Therefore *"Keep it Simple"* and allow the wonderful love and joy of our Creator to fill our spirits and guide our steps.

Grab a Gratitude Not an Attitude

Who has traveled this earth without trials and tribulations? Even Christ cried out to His Father to take the cup away. And it is in our anguish that we are vulnerable and truly "unsafe."

This tool is one of the first "not so nice tools" we will make part of our life. It forces rather than shows. It demands discipline rather than freely giving us peace. And it is one of the first tools of change we will use.

There are two powerful messages here for us and they will fill our lives with a new sense of direction and focus.

First, pain and suffering will continue to happen. There is no magical transportation to another level or world. This indeed was the a key symptom of our DIS-ease and a constant stumbling block for each of us. How many "Beam me up Scotty" bumper stickers have we seen. When will we learn that our trouble will follow us and the human existence will always carry its portion of grief and pain and suffering.

Second, our best response to the times of trouble is to reflect on the good things that have been our gifts from God. *THIS IS NOT A COP OUT OR AN AVOIDANCE TECHNIQUE.* In fact, it is exactly the opposite. It is recognition of who we are and in who's arms we are being carried.

These times of honing and trial are very important in the beginning of the journey because it is so easy to still see the "other pathway" and think it would be better to return to the avoidance of our "other life." We need to build an effective tool that lets us get over the hump of the initial surge of feelings and emotions until our spirit and conscience can refocus and bring us back to our true goal of being in love with Christ.

Easy Does It - But Do It

This little tool is sometimes shortened to "*Easy Does It*". What a wonderful way to get through this world. And how critically close we come to the worldly saying of get it later or put off till tomorrow what we should have done yesterday or someone else will pick up the slack.

"*Easy Does It...But Do It*" needs to be practiced fully to have the proper effect on our journey. It is not an avoidance of the work to be done. It is an understanding that the work is not the center of our focus, our continuing love of Christ is. The work must remain a result of this love.

"*Easy Does It...But Do It*" is a tool used to ease up and stop to smell the roses. We seem to think if we can do it twice as fast we will get twice as much out of it. If we work twice as hard we will receive twice as much. What we need to see in this tool is that the very action of working "extra hard" can become the symptom of our DIS-ease in a new and very dangerous form.

Those of us who have come from a physical malady can point directly at the culprit. But how do we see the culprit in "good works"? How can we discern the tragedy of our lives when we were helping others? My personal experience is filled with these times of true trouble. Neglected family members and friends for the "good and glory of God" is a hollow trophy to hang in one's heart. Especially when that is truly not what Christ asks of us!

So this tool is the admonition to stop the race and allow Christ to perform the wonderful works of His kingdom here on earth. We will be the glad bearers of the oars and He will direct our boat giving us enough to do each day of our lives and the nourishment to do the work comfortably.

Maybe that is a good way to test where we are with this tool. If we are struggling to stay up with the work in front of us, step back and see what it is God wants us to do and what He wants to do for us. Anyway, we need to do our part, but remember that our friend the carpenter from Galilee wants us to enjoy the world He gave His life for. This is His kingdom and He is the God of Love.

First Things First

This is a wonderful way to make the day's work part of our time with Christ. When we take the few moments to evaluate what it is we should do first in the day ahead of us, we begin the process of bringing Christ into our lives on a daily basis.

At First it will seem that this is just another management tool to make things appear in control. Please remember that the tools of the child will grow with the child and will become something special in our maturity. We will look at the physical, worldly things first because they are familiar to us and part of our conscious thoughts. However, slowly we will see Christ's desires for us, and where they fit within our lives.

One of the most positive areas of this tool is teaching the process that Christ will use in guiding our lives. I see His subtle work in us through all the world and not as something apart or foreign to the world.

When we take *"First Things First"* we allow our lives to be built on logical steps of progression. In this structured existence, Christ will place His will for us and we will be able to live a life for Christ.

Expect a Miracle

Of all the little sayings, *"Expect a Miracle,"* most directly identifies the power of the program. This is the acknowledgement of the true power and infinite love of Our Savior in our lives. This is our personal proclamation of our belief in Christ and His kingdom.

At first, it seems to be the most desperate of prayers, and I remember crying out and saying, "prove it if You can!" Now, *having been the recipient of many of His miracles,* it is a wonderful opportunity to tell others of the loving power of my savior. Please, by all means, *"Expect a Miracle"*

But for the Grace of God

✞ Look deeply into the eyes of a suffering elder or a malformed child. What do you feel?

✞ Look at the back of someone departing from the pathway of Christ. How do you react?

✞ See the anger and resentments and hatred and fear in the eyes of one without Christ in their lives. What should you do?

Each of these incidences is real and can be seen, felt and experienced each day of our lives. How do we react to this type of stimuli? How do we cope with the world around us.

This tool, *"But for the Grace of God"*, is the tool of power. Yes power. We have said so many times to ourselves we need Christ in our lives. And now, when we face the most challenging moments of our faith life, we need Him the most.

This is not a statement of "thank God that's not me," it is an understanding that indeed Christ is the center of what we need to be whole.

I cannot accept this as "these people are here to help us on our way," There is no room in my heart or soul or spirit for a god who creates suffering so that I may feel better. No, this is the acknowledgement of our own humanity. We are all the same and there is nothing that separates me from these same maladies or trials except *"the Grace of God."* We need to acknowledge this and understand in the same moment the power He has already bestowed on us through His mercy.

If God Seems Far Away....

It is a wonderful thing to understand that God never.....*NEVER*.....left me in the time of my troubles. Part of the beginning of the program is not to see the faults of our past life but to recognize how and where Christ was helping without our knowledge or even our request for His help.

We will, in our continuing humanity, find more times when we will wonder where Christ is and why He is not taking care of us.

Like the wonderful prayer of the *Footsteps in the Sand*, we will see that Christ will ALWAYS carry us in times of trouble. He will always be there. We need to recognize who is pulling away. In the third step, we will acknowledge this formally as we turn ourselves over to the care of the Lord. Here we will see life as a series of efforts to rest in the care of the Lord, a process of trying to stay as close as possible to Our Savior.

Now we know that if we do not feel God's presence, *WE* moved away from the Lord's constant and eternal care.

Prayers, Poems and a Starting Note

The following poem has captured the heart and minds of many on this journey. I share it now so that you too can be touched by its beautiful message of love.

FOOTPRINTS

One night a man had a dream. He dreamed he was walking along the beach with the LORD. Across the sky flashed scenes from his life. For each scene, he noticed two sets of footprints in the sand; one belonging to him, and the other to the LORD.

When the last scene of his life flashed before him, he looked back at the footprints in the sand. He noticed that many times along the path of his life there was only one set of footprints. He also noticed that it happened at the very lowest and saddest times of his life.

This really bothered him and he questioned the LORD about it. "LORD, you said that once I decided to follow you, you'd walk with me all the way. But I have noticed that during the most troublesome times in my life, there is only one set of footprints. I don't understand why when I needed you most you would leave me?"

The LORD replied. "My precious, precious child. I love you and I would never leave you. During your times of trial and suffering, when you see only one set of footprints, it was then that I carried you.

Margaret Fishback Powers*

* Please take the time to read the wonderful true story about this poem and its author. There is power both in the poem and in the life of Margaret Fishback Powers and her family.

Footprints - The True Story Behind the Poem That Inspires Millions, Harper Collins Publishers Ltd., 1993.

Listen also now to the wonderful words of the following prayer. It holds within it the essence of Christ's message of love and service and the foundation of the 12 Step Program.

PRAYER OF ST. FRANCIS

Lord make me a channel of your peace,
that where there is hatred, I may bring love;
that where there is wrong, I may bring the spirit
    of forgiveness;
that where there is error, I may bring truth;
that where there is doubt, I may bring faith;

that where there is despair, I may bring hope;
that where there are shadows, I may bring light;
that where there is sadness, I may bring joy.

Lord, grant that I may seek rather to comfort than
    to be comforted;
to understand than to be understood;
to love than to be loved.

For it is by giving that one receives.
It is by self-forgetting that one finds.
It is by forgiving that one is forgiven.
And it is by dying that one awakens to eternal
    life.

The Twelve Steps

Now we begin the process. Below we will find all of
the Steps listed together. Read them to get an overall
view of the process.

Step #1 We admitted we were powerless over
_____- that our lives had become
unmanageable.

Step #2 Came to believe that a Power greater than
ourselves could restore us to sanity.

Step #3 Made a decision to turn our will and our lives
over to the care of God *as we understood
Him.*

Step #4 Made a searching and fearless moral
inventory of ourselves.

Step #5 Admitted to God, to ourselves and to another
human being the exact nature of our wrongs.

Step #6 Were entirely ready to have God remove all
these defects of character.

Step #7 Humbly asked Him to remove our
shortcomings.

Step #8   Made a list of all persons we had harmed, and became willing to make amends to them all.

Step #9   Made direct amends to such people wherever possible, except when to do so would injure them or others.

Step #10   Continued to take personal inventory and when we were wrong promptly admitted it.

Step #11   Sought through prayer and meditation to improve our conscious contact with God *as we understood Him,* praying only for the knowledge of His will and the power to carry that out.

Step #12   Having had a spiritual awakening as a result of these Steps, we tried to carry this message to _____, and to practice these principles in all our affairs.

The direct simplicity is hopefully apparent. We should also "feel" a kinship with each and every Step we see here. What will follow is a progressive deepening of each of these Steps within our lives and a clarification of the principles of this process as identified by the steps and scriptures.

WOW! What a mouthful!

Jesus was asked how we could attain the kingdom. He said love one another. The question asked for the last 2000 years is HOW.

Deep in my heart, as witnessed by my experiences, I believe the 12 Steps crystalize this process of love so that Christ can truly work in our lives today and fulfill the answer to the question HOW.

The First Step Process

<table>
<tr><td colspan="4" align="center">STEP #1</td></tr>
<tr><td colspan="4">We admitted we were powerless over _____- that our lives had become unmanageable.</td></tr>
<tr><td colspan="4" align="center">HONESTY</td></tr>
<tr><td colspan="2" align="center">BIG BOOK</td><td colspan="2" align="center">BIBLE</td></tr>
<tr><td>Honesty</td><td>58, 115, 481, 482, 507, 550</td><td>Romans
Mark
Matthew</td><td>7: 13-25
10: 17-22
19: 16-31</td></tr>
<tr><td>Self Will</td><td>60</td><td>John
Exodus</td><td>15: 1-17
20: 3</td></tr>
<tr><td colspan="4">What I do, I do not understand. For I do not do what I want, but I do what I hate.
 Romans 7: 15 </td></tr>
</table>

Welcome to the journey of love and service. Yes, that is what this truly is. Love, because the primary result of this walk will be a relationship with *Jesus Christ* and service, because when we have completed the 12 Steps we will want to share what we have been given in love.

The overall message of the 1st Step is understanding the truth of our life and what we can and cannot control. For most, this is a necessary result of intervention in a disease that has brought a "Bottom" or turning point in our life. However we may define this bottom, we need to find a better way. For those who have chosen the spiritual pathway for the sake of continuing their growth, the "Bottom", while less evident, is the DIS-ease we feel inside with life and the desire to grow beyond these feelings of emptiness. No one will begin this journey unless there is a desire to find something new and better.

I appreciate Philip St. Romain's approach to opening the 1st Step and, with respect, repeat and expand on his work.

The key he brings forward is the parable of the rich man. We have listened to this parable. Have we understood the message? Have we accepted this lesson Christ has given us? Listen once more to Mark 10: 17-22

> As he was setting out on a journey, a man ran up, knelt down before him, and asked him, "Good teacher, what must I do to inherit eternal life?" Jesus answered him, "Why do you call me good? No one is good but God alone. You know the commandments: 'you shall not kill; you shall not commit adultery; you shall not steal; you shall not bear false witness; you shall not defraud; honor your father and your mother.'" He replied to him, "Teacher, all of these I have observed from my youth." Jesus looked at him, loved him and said to him, "you are lacking in one thing. Go sell what you have, and give to the poor and you will have treasure in heaven; then come, follow me." At that statement his face fell, and he went away sad, for he had many possessions.

Now listen with our hearts to these words from Philip St. Romain:

> From this episode in the life of Jesus we learn that legalistic observance of the commandments does not bring deep joy. We also see that Jesus has come not only for those who are broken in health and spirit but also for many who are comfortable and empty. Like the rich young man, however, we must be willing to be honest enough with ourselves to examine our lives to see if we are satisfied or if we yearn for more. Like him too, we must be willing to bring our yearning before Jesus. Unlike him, we must respond in obedience to Jesus' invitation to accept God's gifts of grace in our lives.
>
> (Becoming a New Person - Page 15)

Here is an opening to this 12 Step Process for many Christians. In fact, we would not be remiss in saying All Christians. And please, PLEASE do not walk away because you don't want to open your wallet! That is NOT the message. The message is that, through our human condition, we have a blockage that keeps us from the full grace of God and, because of His most wonderful gift of free choice, we must be the ones to make the first move. The parable of the rich man identifies the yearning within our existence. This is the spiritual nature of our being - our "made in the image and likeness of God" that brings us to want more than the earthly realm. Experience this yearning and allow it to fill our consciousness. It will help to focus both emotional feelings and physical needs as part of our spiritual nature. The rich man proves what we already know, but like him, have difficulty accepting. Physical and emotional fulfillment will not satisfy us if we do not satisfy our spiritual needs.

A point of caution

One of the overriding principles of the 12 Step Program is *"progress rather than perfection."* We cannot and must not allow this 1st Step to overpower our chance for spiritual change.

1.   This 1st Step is an invitation to honesty. It requires no change.
2.   The 12 Step process and the principles of Christianity do not require perfection. To expect perfection from ourselves is to take the place of God and miss the goal of this process all together.
3.   We are not called to give up life. We are invited to enhance it!

My personal experience brought me to the 12 Steps out of life threatening and dire need, (or so I thought). Once the symptom of the disease was removed I found an empty vessel with grave longings for love and fulfillment. The choices presented were to build and enhance my spiritual nature or to crawl back into the bottle. My faltering and childlike first steps within the program brought me closer to a personal relationship with my Higher Power. This principle of self honesty and truth about my spiritual nature brought more fulfillment, more joy, more meaning, more peace than any bottle ever did! I did not give up the bottle - I received Christ!

Please Mr. Rich Man. Listen to the yearning within your very soul. You will not give up your wealth. You will gain MUCH MUCH MORE!

This part of the process and the beginning of the whole journey is based upon the honest acknowledgement of our place in life. It is in this effort that we find our position with Christ and within His kingdom here on earth. Here we come to understand both our needs and wants. Here we come to grips with Christ and, in doing so, find true solace.

Preparation

Powerless over "_____"

As we are to deal with Spirituality, there needs to be a moment taken for filling in the blank in this step. We need to identify where exactly our powerlessness exists within our life and name the DIS-ease that holds us captive. This need not be catastrophic and need not be physically life threatening. In my opinion, spiritual addiction can be more draining on us than any physical or mental malady.

For me and many others the word "SIN" fills in the blank and gives focus to the process of the 12 Steps. We can define sin as the absence of control over doing things against our better judgement. Over time we will enhance this definition (with the help of Christ) and broaden our understanding of our powerlessness.

How deeply do we seek?

Like the beginning of these writings, we did not delve into the Steps right away. Here too, we do not want to try to find the depth of any malady when we have just begun the process.

If we are to await the final outcome of our Christianity, we most likely will never be able to find Christ in this life. It is the same here with the identification of our DIS-ease. We have grave choices, to accept what we know and move on or wait for the final outcome and maybe loose life in the meantime. What we need to know at this stage is not the why and how but that our life is not in control; that our existence is not filled with peace and serenity as it should be; that we are not whole.

We are like the rose. As the petals of our life and meaning open up there is wonderful beauty. However, if we wait until all the petals are reveled, we will be next to death and no longer will the true beauty of our existence be evident. The mystery is that Christ has given us life, not the answer but the process. Now we are going to identify the parts of the process that are broken and unmanageable, not seek the answer to life.

Note that it is possible to "miss" something we need to know about ourselves. But rest in this fact from one who has traveled this path with many a "missed something." Jesus with wonderful love and boundless care, will watch over us and help us find rest within His arms.

The Truth Inside

The following exercise is to help us find the center of our honesty which is the principle of this 1st Step.

Three major points are addressed by this exercise:

1.   We can be totally honest within the safety of ourselves.
2.   Truth is an "inside" reality. We can find the answer we seek.
3.   If something is wrong, we will feel it inside.

Truth Inside Exercise

Now gently and quietly focus your being. Close your eyes and let your mind and body and spirit be at rest. I have yet to meet the person who, in this state, cannot find the true voice of their being. (In the Big Book it does describe those unfortunates who cannot be completely honest with themselves.) We are not among those unfortunates. We have the ability to be honest and have the opportunity to allow honesty to lead us in this moment of truth. There is no conflict in this place of "self", there is no quiz or required testament to strangers. We are speaking only to ourselves and we are free to "voice" the pain within knowing we can protect ourselves from outside control and influence.

For many this voice has been defined as our conscience. For some this is the voice of reason working within us. So many times we have been told as children not to talk to ourselves. Now we are going to toss away this misconception and listen to ourselves in honesty and openness.

Setting Our Personal Goals

For this part of the process we will focus only on short term goals. There is an essential nature in humanity that requires food before effort and at this stage in the spiritual search we need to be fed not taught deep theological laws.

Here are the three goals suggested at this time,

> Short Term:
> 1. Opening the mind to possibilities
> 2. Feeling the feelings
> 3. Accepting who I am

Opening the mind to possibilities

As with all processes, there is no isolated step. We will be seeing and feeling many of the principles of Steps 2 through 12 as we work this 1st Step. It is usual to feel the entire process but we will attempt to stay focused on the Step at hand. What we look for, here, is concentration and focus on this portion of the process. In this way, we can instill the essence of the Step within our lives and make it part of our personal principles.

Father John Powell, S.J. calls this the "Life Principle" (*Unconditional Love*, Chapter 1). Each of us owns a center of being from which we can operate. This center is where our current Life Principle dwells. It is here that the search must begin.

Like the "Truth Inside Exercise" above, we need to enter into our "self" and understand the motives of our actions. This is the center of our being and, if we have pain or DIS-ease, this is the center of our malady. We can change our "Life Principle." We can make a new and more focused start on our spiritual journey. But we need to know where we are in order to begin. The 1st Step is the actualization of our beginning. It is not condemnation. It is not defeat. It is an honest assessment of where we are on the spiritual path so that we can proceed to where we want to be.

Now maybe the statement of "this is a program for those who want it, not those who need it" makes some sense. Ours is not the defeat of our past but the wonderful rejoicing in the things to come!

Feeling the feelings

Now is the time to set the first definition of our journey. *Feelings are not right or wrong, they just are.* We need to feel them and acknowledge them for their reality and we need to set them in front of us so that we can know them and their effects on our past life. Please note the term "past life." One of the benefits of the journey will be to restructure how we deal with feelings in the future so that we do not approach another "bottom."

For now we need to just identify them and their effects on our life. We see the world and are aware of its stimuli. These are feelings, neither right or wrong, they just are. Our humanity has been given the gift of feelings so we can interpret and understand the world around us.

For most, there is a body of experiential events that have placed categories for these feelings. One of the best I know is HATE. Remember back in "the good old days." It was a sin to HATE. (Now stay with me here, there is sin involved.) I felt I was evil every time the feeling of hatred arose in my being. The feeling is not the sin. The conscious decision to act on this hatred is the evil. Now we will focus on these feelings of our personal life and see them for what they are.

When my security was attacked by anyone, I would retaliate and blame or ridicule them. The feeling was "fear of insecurity." Through the process of the 12 Steps, I have reformed my "Life Principle" and now can control the reaction to the feeling of insecurity! It is still there, but my focus and control is very different.

Please note:

> We are not attempting to delve into the depths of our "reactions" now. That part of the process will come later. First we must build a foundation upon which we can stand in security and true peace.

Accepting who I am

> A man walked into the town and found a child dirty and crying in the mud by the side of the road.
>
> With no words, he stopped and sat beside the child spreading mud all over himself. The child stopped its tears and began to laugh at the man. "Why are you doing such a silly thing?" asked the child. The man looked at the child and said "I wanted to see if it would make me cry."
> Again the child laughed and said, "I'm crying because I feel unhappy inside."
>
> "What could cause such unhappiness in a child," said the man.
>
> "I don't know," said the child as the tears reappeared on its cheeks.
>
> "Has the mud helped you find your feelings?"
>
> "No, that's silly," said the child.
>
> "Then maybe we should try another game to help us find your feelings," replied the man and he offered a hand to the child to stand.

Mud is such a wonderful thing. Always loved by children hated by parents and misunderstood by everyone. So it is with feelings. Our feelings get us into the biggest "mud puddles" where the feelings become the reality and the problem is lost in the mud. The first critical understanding is that something must change if we are to change the feelings within.

To understand the feelings we need to stand back from our present and past life and take an honest look. This "unemotional look" will give us the opportunity for true dramatic change, or at least a vision of the path to take for this change.

The understanding of self is a project that all forms of science and social programs have attempted to control. Here, instead, we choose acceptance. There is nothing wrong with the scientific methods used. We are going to approach our inner self in a different fashion, that is all.

We all know that, unlike the child in the mud, we cannot let feelings hold sway within our lives. We know that we need to have some form of control over our environment. But how do we break free from the constant cycle of cause and effect? How do we break free from the cycle of pain and discontent? How will this Step answer any of the questions that invade our minds and dominate our lives?

The best way is to look at the differences between understanding and acceptance.

Understand: To comprehend; to realize; to know the feeling and thoughts of.

Accept: To take what is given; to believe to be true; to agree.

Both carry the task of seeing the event or feeling or action or dilemma. Only one takes action on this newly found knowledge. So many times we have seen the error of our ways. But have we accepted the error as ours? Have we taken hold of the yoke and placed the blame for our failures where it belongs? This is the honesty and courage required of the 1st Step of the program. This is the change from mud to reality we need to make to transcend the cause and effect cycle our lives get stuck in.

The Discipline

This time in our life is not one filled with joy and emotional excitement. We, as humans, find this "looking within" very somber and quite disturbing. No one goes to the doctor hoping to find a great malady. Yet the very act of going indicates something is wrong.

The basic principle of HONESTY needs to be kept in the forefront of our mind throughout the process of this step. We need to maintain a true communication with ourselves so that we can see the malady for what it is, and not hide it through another round of self-denial.

Our universal DIS-ease maintains a facade that "change" will be more painful than continuance in the DIS-ease. Here is where we need to concentrate our honesty. We have heard the words "walk a mile in my shoes." This has always been the way to help people make changes their very humanity will resist. Now we need to be open to the walk. We need to allow ourselves the ability to see the other side. We need to stand up from our mud puddle and look at the rest of the world in a new light.

I have always said, if we are not happy and do not know where happiness is, then we will have to follow a path we have not taken before. This is the beginning of that journey and it is the marker that identifies the fork in the road.

Now we have a step that will formalize the beginning of that process. Now we have a starting point we can rely on to begin our new life. Now we have the opportunity to honestly try on Christ as the better way of life.

There are many methods available for this fundamental review of our experiences. Many on the 12 Step Journey relate "trouble to DIS-ease". In this way we create a series of experiential events that point to the area within our lives that needs change. I firmly believe this is a good and appropriate method. In the spiritual journey it might look like this:

Troubling Event	My Feelings of Where God Was / Is	My faults / areas of need
Not being able to fit into the social group at work.	God really doesn't care how happy I am.	I do not trust God to guide my life.
Pain felt in being overweight.	He doesn't care if I hurt.	My inability to control my eating habits.
Aggravation over work and bosses.	God never cared about my job or how I supported my family.	My job is something I do not allow God into.
Being bored on Sunday at Church	God is not there for me anymore.	Assuming God is supposed to make my life happy.
Finding out my wife is going to leave me.	There is no God! He can't love me.	I just do not know the true meaning of love.
.....	.....	.....

Each of these events are real and part of my life. The feelings, please remember, are not good or bad they just are. Most important is the honest refection of where I fit in on each of these events. Where I have failed in my union with Christ. It is here that the acceptance takes place. It is here that the keys to the change will be found.

Now remember, I do not look for answers yet. And, PLEASE GOD, make each of us understand that we, although in pain, are safe here to express what really needs to be said.

We are HONESTLY looking at our REAL EXPERIENCES and stating the FACTS of our life and faith and needs.

We have an "un-manageability" that causes pain and discontent. Now is the time to work on changing the "un-manageability." Now is the time to find a new path in life. Now is the time to start down the path once traveled by a carpenter's son from Galilee.

A few thoughts on this Step.

Time:
> Time is not the factor that will decide when we are ready to go on. Time is a gift from God, and we may use it as we see fit.

The Goal:
> My sponsor once told me the story of the man from a southern country who needed to go north.

After all the preparation and planning the man walked out of his house and faced north.

My sponsor then asked me where the man was with regards to his goal? My answer was "far away."

The truth, my sponsor related, was that the man was on his journey and therefore fully in line with his goal, for it is not the destination it is the journey.

So we have begun our journey. We have identified the truth within our lives. Now let us seek to find the truth about Jesus Christ.

The Second Step Process

STEP #2

Came to believe that a Power greater than ourselves could restore us to sanity.

HOPE

BIG BOOK	BIBLE	
Hope (Willingness)	Psalm	131
12-13, 26, 46-47, 53,	Romans	1: 16-17
57, 60, 69, 70, 79, 93,	2 Timothy	1: 6-20
118, 124, 152, 153,	Matthew	28: 16-20
158-159, 162	Mark	12: 28-34
		10: 51-52

Psalm 131 - Humble Trust in God

LORD, my heart is not proud;
nor are my eyes haughty.
I do not busy myself with great matters,
with things too sublime for me.
Rather, I have stilled my soul,
hushed it like a weaned child.
Like a weaned child on its mother's lap,
so is my soul within me.
Israel, hope in the LORD,
now and forever.

I have always found this the *"quiet step"* and will approach it as such here. I also know from deep, profound, personal experience that this is one of the most powerful steps in the program.

Preparation

I ask that, in your individual journey, you take the time to open up to this step so that you may feel the real power of the Lord and know that the rest of the work is, for you, the best way to Our Creator.

The preparation of this step is not totally of our doing. In fact, our part is to become available. We present ourselves openly to hear, see and feel God within our lives. Too many times we have forced faith down our own throats. We have decided how we will believe and how we will act as Christians. For many of us this is out of a sense of urgency to be close to our God. A desirable goal, but have we been able to attain it? Many, many times the answer is no. Now we will attempt a different approach to the process of belief.

We will not create a new religion. We will not separate ourselves from the traditional beliefs of our ancestors. We will not find a different God than the one of our childhood. We will open our souls to the wonders of our Savior, Jesus Christ, and let Him fill us with the gift of belief.

This may sound like a bunch of word games but let us, for a moment in the journey, allow a new light to shine within the sanctuary of our spirits.

Setting Our Personal Goals

Our goals here will be set as short term and very immediate. We are going to set up a system of cause and response that we can use to measure Christ's power. (Now don't walk out just yet. This is truly not blasphemy!) What we will do is look at where Christ has touched us and see if this is something we want, something we need, and something we truly like.

Here are the three goals suggested at this time:

> Short Term:
> 1. Seeking the power in our lives
> 2. Finding Christ in this power
> 3. Confirming His presence

Too many times we say we believe but still cower in the darkness of our unbelief. Listen to the meditation from Karen Albertus:

Faith is a gift. It is not simply a matter of willpower, of being willing to trust. God can increase that faith, deepen it.

A man asks Jesus to cure his epileptic son, if He "can."

Jesus said to him, " 'If you can!' Everything is possible to one who has faith." Then the boy's father cried out, "I do believe, help my unbelief!"
Mark 9:23-24

Even if we only want to believe, we can ask for an increase in faith, for, somehow, wanting is the seed of believing.

Here we can see very clearly what it is we need to do. This is a time of opening our spirits and our souls and our minds to the wonders of Christ directly related to our lives. We cannot find the power or the promises of this program if we do not truly believe that Christ makes a difference in our personal lives. He cannot be someone who helps others but not us. He cannot be someone apart from our world and our lives. He cannot be someone who allows us to live and die in a fate we can not control.

This is not a program of sitting around and letting God fall into our laps. It needs to be a personal journey with real feelings and real thought. Now is indeed the time for us to think and feel what it is to be one of God's children. What it is to be intimately loved by Jesus Christ, to touch the very existence of His love for us and in the moment He offers Himself up for us?

Here's a thought:
> The next time you sing a song like "I have a friend in Jesus" listen to your heart and see if you really believe the words. Test your faith in the quiet safety of your mind and heart and soul. See where you stand with the power of the Lord. Is your soul the child nestled in the arms of your Mother God, or are you standing alone and on your own?

I have made a point to set only short term goals. We will always practice each of these steps and there are long term goals to be set. However, there is a real need to focus on the "here and now" within this step in order to assure we are truly prepared to move on.

In my own experience I found this when I attempted the 3rd Step. Running merrily along the wonderful path of the program, I came to the "time of official acceptance." I was going to throw myself into the loving arms of my Creator and be "happy, joyous and free" forever more. The excitement built and the wonder of feeling God so powerfully in me was awesome. I could not wait to become a saint! I could not wait to be in the arms of my God! I remember how long the days seemed as the time ticked slowly towards that Wednesday when I would take my 3rd Step.

Then the pain. Then the doubt. And the age-old problem of humanity filled me with dread, drowning out all the joy and wonder of the Lord. I began to realize that I did not know or believe in this Christ. I was not ready to jump off any cliff with the wonderful expectations of a child knowing my Father will catch me. I did not have faith.

It still hurts today to realize how deeply I needed Jesus to hold me and how unable I was to allow Him the chance. My sadness was great enough that, for a moment, I thought the journey had turned into another emotional ride to nowhere. Once again, I was alone and there was no hope for me. One more time I had followed a dream and come up empty.

This is a time when I can attest to the power of the tools of the program. I was told not to make any major decisions within the first year. (In fact my sponsor, fully aware of the care and guidance I needed, allowed my first decision upon my anniversary in the program to be "not to make any decisions for another year.") Broken and without hope I sought out my sponsor to inform him of my pending doom. Melodramatic as it was, I went to tell him that I would not be able to stay around for the promises, that I could not take the 3rd Step. I figured I was one of the "constitutionally incapable" and would have to live out my life in pain and suffering and DIS-ease.

I don't remember too many times when my sponsor didn't have an acid filled retort to my childish antics. His normal dry humor and sarcasm was set aside in this moment. He simply told me it was OK and I was just where I needed to be! He then, gently and lovingly led me back to the wonderful words of the 2nd Step.

And now, like a small child hurt from my adventures, I tried to truly believe that Jesus would love me. I began the most powerful and filling experiences of my little life. I found hope and safety once more for me. Truly for me!

I love you Jesus. I love you Bill S.

The Discipline

We have come from a step that is filled with a great deal of soul searching and hard core honesty. While we do not sit and "relax", we do try to let God do God's part in our journey.

Here we are to "come to believe." We do not "choose to believe." We do not "force belief." We come to the realization of our true belief. Therefore the major discipline and focus of this step is to allow Christ to show Himself to us personally, in words and deeds that we can understand and accept.

So many miss the power and fortification of this step because they accept their past beliefs or the beliefs of others. When, with a little time and openness, we can allow God to be revealed to us in a personal and soul filling relationship.

Important Point:
> **We must be ready to understand the previous statement. This is in no way a condemnation of the traditions of the Christians who have preceded us on this journey.**
>
> **Here we are looking at the misdirection of our own faith and the problem of blind acceptance of the ways of others. These are the two areas we need to change. Most of us on this journey find the same God we have always known, but we now find we can be part of the Creator's world fully and joyfully.**

It may be easier to see it this way. If we are truly involved with a Savior who cares deeply for us as an individual and seeks our personal relationship, then we should be able to assume that He will show this to us. In this step, therefore, we allow this revealing to happen.

When the founders of this program included the 2nd Step it was to help the wounded children see a new dawn. They were not interested in wealth and power. They wanted to help those in deep pain and suffering to see the smallest amount of HOPE that God really did care. Listen to some of the ways they tell others to see God in their lives:

> When you ate breakfast this morning was it good? Can you remember a time when you could not even think of food in the morning? Who helped you find a way to this nourishment?

> How many days did you spend in loneliness? Look around at the friends who truly care for you and your journey. Who helped you find this place of recovery?

> Think of how you felt in the mornings when you awoke drunk and in jail. How did you feel this morning when you awoke home, safe and secure? Who did that for you?

Hope is not something we can get from someone else. No matter how unafraid of today they are, we need to find our own hope, our own peace of mind. We need to have our own personal understanding of Christ. The discipline of this step is to take the time to search through our past and present and see where Christ has touched our lives. Then with mind and emotion and spirit we allow these true, personal events to become the foundation of our "new belief." We come to the fully personal acceptance that Jesus has been and is and will be a loving and caring part of our lives.

Look back to the tools of our program and see how they have been pointing us towards this moment in our journey. Look deeply into the very process of this program and see how it has carried us until we could see that it was Jesus all along.

Look deeply within, to the voice we opened up to in the 1st Step, and ask these basic questions:

☦   Is this real or just another emotional roller-coaster bound for doom?
☦   Is this what I have searched for through DIS-ease and other faith attempts or is this just another program without results?
☦   Is it truly possible that Jesus loves me?

Of all the tools I would recommend in this part of the journey it is "KISS" (Keep It Simple and Steady). Now is not the time to try to move mountains, now is the time to see the roses and look once more at the simple beauty around us. What child is interested in solving the tremendous problems of the world? What God would make that a requirement of our recovery or acceptance of the journey? For today "KISS," and allow

Him to show His wonderful healing powers to us as we would want to show a little child how much we love them.

Here, my friends, is the essence of the child's heart. Here is the powerful "Quiet Step" that builds the strength of the foundation which will not be torn down. Here is the place of true growth and happiness. Here is the gift of personal HOPE in the Lord and the powers of life this HOPE gives us through Jesus Christ.

The Third Step Process

FAITH

BIG BOOK	BIBLE	
Spiritual Experience	John	3: 16-17
569-570	Matthew	14: 22-33
	Psalm	91:14-16
Serenity 68, 544, 551,	James	2: 14-26
552		

Whoever clings to me I will deliver;
whoever knows my name I will set on high.

All who call upon me I will answer;
I will be with them in distress;
I will deliver them and give them honor.

With length of days I will satisfy them
and show them my saving power.
                                        Psalm 91: 14-16

And now, with the inner delight of having worked diligently to reach this juncture in our journey, we make ready for the kingdom of the Lord. I have never seen this Step fail to bring beauty, and grace, and love, and reason to those who choose to accept its grace. I have never seen anyone who has come this far that has not received some of the promises of the program. This is, I believe, a fully documented process of *FAITH WITH PROMISES TO MAKE IT REAL.*

Looking into the doorway of the 3rd Step, there is no need to pause, because we have been appropriately prepared for the gifts to be received. Come and join those who have gone before us to mark the pathway into Jesus' loving arms.

Preparation

It is hopeful that, by this time, we will realize that it is not a faith leap into a chasm of the unknown. By now, we have become more than ready to run into the arms of our loving and caring Father God, we are yearning for the rest within the embrace of our Mother God.

Preparation is therefore simple and quickly accomplished.

Set aside some time to share this moment with others on the journey, choose a gift we will give to ourselves for the work that we have done, and obtain permission from our sponsor to take the step.

The sharing will meet the needs of the community and help others find their way to the place we have come. The gift is the first indication to ourselves that we have truly progressed and this is part of the goodness of His kingdom. The sponsor - well let us talk about the sponsor.

Sponsorship

There have always been travelers along the road of spiritual growth who have taken this journey alone and in solitude. These are the special ones and they have done much for the Lord in their solitary steps. We, however, look to community and a pathway with others to guide and be guided. This is where most of the sainthood will be found and we need to open ourselves to the graces of this community.

Sponsorship, as a philosophical ideal, can be looked at as the personal commitment to walk with the community. We, as individuals, choose to align ourselves with the group by becoming subject to the traditions of the group and allowing others to show us the way. This subjugation is one way we have of making ourselves part of the body of Christ. Resistance to a sponsor normally shows areas where we do not want to open ourselves and release our selfish ways. These, indeed, can be the grounds where sin maintains its hold.

Important Point:

We need to be sure of one thing. Guides show the path they have traveled. They **NEVER** impose their own path on those they sponsor. While a sponsor may pray heartily for one who is having difficulty with a step, they let God do

God's work! The sponsor shares their experience to help soften the road for the one they serve.

What is Sponsorship

First: It is the sharing of our current life with another individual who has the ability to understand *because they have already experienced what we are going through*. We should be able to see a difference between a sponsor and a teacher.

✝   *A teacher* has the knowledge and may or may not have the experience. A teacher takes on the responsibility of passing on the truth.

✝   *The sponsor* does not take on this role of instruction. They lead by their own example and only offer what it is they have experienced.

Second: Opening up to a sponsor can only be done *when we have built up a level of trust*. We need to be fully aware that we share our lives when we are ready with those we can trust with our personal information.

It is a very scary reality to think about picking a sponsor. Our thoughts go directly to the 5th Step of the program and we naturally choke. Remember where we are. How long has it been since we trusted anyone? When was the last time we had any form of valued confidence?

We will open up when it is time because we will be prepared to open up and we will have prepared our sponsor to receive our life. Think of the natural release of tension and pain when we were held in our parents arms and cried out our wounds of childhood. This outlet has been taken away from our Christian life style and we are sadly lacking this wonderful grace. Know that over time and through the process of these 12 Steps we will re-find this wonderful avenue of healing and share openly and freely and joyfully with our properly prepared sponsor.

Third: We will use our sponsor in the most critical self seeking parts of our 12 Step process. The 6th and 7th Steps require a great deal of insight and many changes. Our sponsor will provide two avenues of assistance:

> 1. They will use the basic information of the 4th and 5th Step (sponsors forget the details very very quickly) to provide the starting ground for our new life changes, pointing to character defects and shortcomings of the past to help us focus on the changes we want in our new life.

> 2. Then they will be there to be a reflection of our progress in this new and wonderful process.

Self Discipline is achieved by becoming a disciple of someone who has gone before us. Now we all know that we follow Christ and that He will always remain the true shepherd. But we must also see that He uses others to reach us and help us to grow in His love and service. This is the true role of the sponsor.

How Do We Pick a Sponsor:

For those of us in dire need of healing and recovery we were told:

✞   "We should select our sponsor the same way we would select a bathroom when the urgent need arises!

- AND -

✞   Remember that this is not a marriage and we can change sponsors if we need to. For now, we get someone who can show us the path of spirituality."

This I know from my life experience and will help guide your choice. Ask your potential sponsor the following:

✞   Have you made the 12 Steps a part of your life? (Do you walk the walk not just talk the talk?)

✞   Will you have time to share your experience, strength and hope with me?

✞   Can I have the right to open up to you as I am ready and not on your timetable?

With these questions answered positively you will be well on the way to building a good sponsorship relationship.

Remember, once more, that the process of the Steps will help us decide the right time to share our life and help us in selecting the right person for our sharing. Now we need only open up to what the sponsor can offer us. Think of the wonderful ministry of Jesus. Isn't that exactly what He did for us. He shared His fullness and life until we were ready to open up to Him.

Welcome to the wonderful pathway of Christian sponsorship.

What are my responsibilities? What are the sponsor's?

I believe that these responsibilities are one in the same so I will answer them together.

✞ Sharing
Remember the process and remember that as we grow our sharing will grow. It is wonderful to see the change from the silent newcomer and talkative sponsor to the open communication of those on the journey together. It will come as we build our relationship of trust and Christian love.

✞ Listening
At first this may be all we can do. This is OK. It is said to the newcomers, "God gave you two ears and one mouth. Take the cotton out of your ears and stuff it in your mouth!" Maybe a bit radical but listening is a lost art in our world and now is the time to learn its benefits.

✝ Helping ourselves
    Sponsors truly enjoy the process of
    sponsorship. We are not and never will be a
    burden. Sponsorship is the direct means by
    which sponsors grow in their own program. It
    is a very selfish and centered decision on the
    part of the sponsor. To continue to grow in
    spirituality WE MUST GIVE IT AWAY.

    Early in the AA program Bill W. found himself
    looking into a bar at the Akron Hotel. When
    he fought through this urge and instead
    reached out to another in need he realized one
    the most profound messages of Christ. We are
    Christians by our love and we can only
    maintain this love through service to others.

And so my friends I end this note on Sponsorship. It is
the life blood of the 12 Step process and the carrier of
the unique and dynamic traditions of the program. Keep
this in mind, and focus on what a sponsor can bring to
us. This will enable us to trust more readily, and quickly
use the ingrained traditions of the journey for our
benefit.

Setting Our Personal Goals

Our goals will be for today and the rest of the journey.
This step is returned to more often than any other step
within the program. It contains it a process of "letting

go and letting God" that will remain meaningful and vibrant throughout our lives. So now we will set both short and long term goals:

> Short Term:
> 1. Making a decision
> 2. Understanding God's care
> 3. Gifting myself
>
> Long Term:
> 1. Commitment to a new way
> 2. Continuation of the growth process

What is sought through this step is the *Simplicity of Faith.* We want to set ourselves in the loving arms of our Creator and we will accomplish this with a personal faith built through the previous two steps. Further, as we grow in the knowledge and depth of the program's process we will enhance this *Faith* while maintaining simplicity or the child-like heart.

Listen first to this definition of *Saving Faith*:

> *Saving Faith* is the acceptance by the intellect, affection, and will of God's favor extended to us through Christ.

This definition works to sum up the first three steps of the program. For many of us, this was the "Faith Leap" we were required to make from the beginning moments of our faith experience. We were not given the Steps to come to this decision point of resting in the arms of Christ. What I would like to focus on is the gifting of

God's grace and how we can "choose" this gift. This is the essence of the 3rd Step and the fulfillment of the Step over time within our personal spiritual journeys.

So I approach faith with a requirement for simplicity. When we, as children of God, approach faith only through knowledge or deep theological pondering, we tend to miss the central gifting we receive from the Lord. That is the empowerment of love in our lives. However, when we maintain the child's heart and openness during our spiritual decision, we gain both the knowledge and the empowerment of Christ's special grace.

My reasoning for concentration on simplicity:

✝   We need to make sure the message is from God and not from our own interpretation of God.

✝   We can not or should not stop the progress of our journey until we have the quintessential choice built through study and knowledge.

Both reasons create a sense of urgency to this step. But listen to how the step is described in the "3rd Step Prayer" from the Big Book:

> "God, I offer myself to Thee - to build with me and to do with me as Thou wilt. Relieve me of the bondage of self, that I may better do Thy will. Take away my difficulties, that victory over them may bear witness to those I would help of Thy power, Thy Love, and Thy Way of Life.
>
> May I do Thy will always!"

This urgency is not the type built upon fear, but the longing for the gifts Christ has ready for us just for the asking. It is in this attitude we want to approach the 3rd Step. And so we approach, not the altar of some supreme being way above us, but the open door to our Lord's house knowing God awaits us with open and loving arms.

The Discipline

Discipline seems such a hard word for such a wonderful step. There is need for such discipline in our lives in order to make this step part of our everyday experience.

First, we want to make sure that our attitude of self reliance is replaced with an acknowledgement of God's position in our lives. "We have a new Employer.... Being all powerful, He provides what we need..." it states in the Big Book. This attitude of placing our lives into God's hands is something that will take practice.

Normally we are able to "Let Go" of things only after we have tried "our way" first. The 3rd Step builds a new approach to handling day to day events and challenges in our lives. We bring ALL to God first and find what we are to work on and what God will handle. This allows God's grace to enter into all the work we do and gives us the best chance for a peaceful and filling life.

Second, we will need to grow in our commitment to the Way of Christ. The 3rd Step is the beginning not the end of the faith building journey. We will be transformed by Christ throughout our lives so that we become more pleasing to Him. Like this forging, the decision made in the 3rd Step is the acknowledgement of the beginning of His grace for us and not the fulfillment of His kingdom within our lives. The 12 Step process makes this very clear if we look ahead to the 7th Step. We again commit ourselves to Christ in a similar way but with greater commitment. Again in the 11th and 12th Steps we rededicate ourselves to the "Way of Christ" in ever growing understanding and faith.

Lastly, we need to understand and continue to grow in childhood joy received from the gift of God's love. This may be the most important at this time of the journey. We will continue to approach our Savior and we will continue to learn and understand and commit to His ways. Throughout this Step, all the following steps and indeed throughout our lives we need to maintain the joy of this gift of love from Jesus. It is much too easy for us as humans in search of God to become wrapped up in the search and miss the essence of the journey. Jesus Christ was, is, and always will be. Jesus Christ died for us and freed us from our sins. Jesus Christ founded His kingdom here on earth and swore to protect it and enshure its growth. Jesus Christ is the GOOD NEWS and is real to us today! If we have no joy in our journey then we are, in my humble opinion, looking for a false god. The kingdom of God is now and we are His chosen ones. Rejoice!

In Closing
I have shared with you the time in my life when I could not approach this step and how I had to return to the 2nd Step. Now let me tell you of the wonders I have received when I made the decision to turn my will and life over to God's care.

There was still a sense of question as to my preparedness, yet I knew deeply that the door was now truly open. While I wondered about the mechanics of the "ceremony" I would participate in, I also began to feel a new anticipation. I wanted to get into the Lord's arms. I wanted my Father to hold me. I was bringing up old hidden feelings of my earthly father's love from childhood and longing for the same from God.

The evening arrived and, after our normal Wednesday meeting, I was directed to the back room. Inside the room I found friends and the "elders" of the group greeting me with smiles and warm looks of acceptance. They knew what was to take place and seemed to be filled with joy. I was immediately comforted and relaxed, letting the event happen.

Bill S. spoke first. "By entering that door, you have made your decision. Now you are in the loving care of your Higher Power." Others then shared their personal experiences with both this ceremony and how this 3rd Step had filled their lives. One by one they confirmed and edified the feelings I was having. One by one they gave reality and support to the faith yearnings I held within my heart. One by one they opened the doorway to Christ more and more until I was standing there before Him, the Savior I had sought. I remember Bill asking me how I felt and, stumbling over a few words, I fell silent. His smile broadened and he announced to those around the table that "We have finally broken through the thick skull of this child. I think now he will be able to learn and grow." We all brought the event to a close by saying the 3rd Step Prayer. The emotions were now peeking and I could only follow the words with whispers as I let all reality of the moment sink into my very soul. There before me was my Creator, holding His arms open to me and gently folding me within His embrace. Whatever was to happen in the days and years to come no longer seemed the same within my soul. I was in a different place and a new world. I was home.

Please receive this Step with all the joy and wonderment of a child at Christmas. It has always been God's joy to watch us in the essence of the joy that comes from the Creator's heart. Christ has given us the initial tools to touch and see and feel God's love. Our Lord now wants us to accept this love with the faith of one who has found rest and protection.

This step, above all the rest, is outwardly touched by the spirit of Jesus. He will reveal Himself to you in His care for you! Come, join those who rest safe in the arms of the Creator!

The Fourth Step Process

STEP #4

Made a searching and fearless moral inventory of ourselves.

COURAGE

BIG BOOK		BIBLE	
Fear	67-68, 115, 116	Romans	12: 1 - 8
		Psalm	139
		1 John	1: 5 -10

Now this is the message that we have heard from Him and proclaim to you: God is light, and in Him there is no darkness at all. If we say, "We have fellowship with Him," while we continue to walk in the darkness, we lie and do not act in truth. But if we walk in the light as He is in the light, then we have fellowship with one another, and the blood of His Son Jesus cleanses us from all sin. If we say, "We are without sin," we deceive ourselves, and the truth is not in us. If we acknowledge our sins, He is faithful and just and will forgive our sins and cleanse us from every wrongdoing. If we say, "We have not sinned," we make Him a liar, and His word is not in us.

1 John 1: 5-10

A time has come for a concentrated effort of Honesty, Openness and Willingness. Before beginning, it is important to set ourselves within the framework of the program and reflect on why this step is not the 1st Step.

The 4th Step is the beginning of the end for the past and the burdens we have carried throughout our lives which do not belong to us.

For many Christians, the receiving of the 4th and 5th Steps is an emotionally charged event in front of a congregation receiving immediate salvation and professing our humiliating past to the crowd. This, in essence has made the 4th and 5th Step the 1st Step to recovery within our the Christian church tradition. The salvation is real and right and correct. The humble offering of ones sins to the community is just and scriptural and traditionally appropriate. *The timing is ALL WRONG!*

Preparation

For the most part, the preparation has been the preceding three steps. We have given our minds, bodies and spirits the chance to rest within Our Savior's arms and to assure us that He is real and that He will protect and care for us. We need to reflect on the beauty and the "life giving" experiences we have already received from Our Lord, seeing the benefit of His work within us and then looking to what we can do to help solidify this new union with Jesus. Hopefully we already see that *the timing is NOW RIGHT!* Now we stand before the altar of the Lord and our community and can truly confess with both understanding and true peaceful joy.

Look at promises three and five from the AA Big Book listed in the front of this book. There is to be no regret of the past. Our confession will be used and be pleasing to God as we share it to help others find His forgiveness. Can we see how the whole process of salvation is focused within the order of these steps? The 4th Step is of paramount importance to each and every Christian, but its power and grace cannot be fully realized if we are not prepared by Christ's fullness of love first.

The preceding comments tend to lump Steps 4 and 5 together and they work as a pair within the process. Now we will concentrate on step four and its preparation.

Confirmation of our wholeness and peacefulness received from the 3rd Step will provide a good platform on which to begin the process of the 4th Step. Keep in mind, or even write down, the words of the 3rd Step Prayer. Because if we are in the arms of our Savior, we cannot be harmed by anything, least of all our own confession to our Lord.

Get pencil and paper and find a place of privacy and comfort so that you can begin the task.

Setting Our Personal Goals

There are both short and long term goals to this step. While I am a practitioner of doing this Step once, (the 10th Step takes care of the future needs), the opening of one's very soul honestly and humbly will have far reaching effects on our journey.

> Short Term:
> 1. Completing the process of Honesty
> 2. Final acceptance of ones own life
>
> Long Term:
> 1. The open kimono principle
> 2. The inward watch for new DIS-ease

In the short term there is a definite, powerful and critical event taking place. We are going to fully surrender to ourselves and to honesty. We are going to set aside the DIS-ease related symptoms of blocking and excuses and "but." We are going to take on the cloak of honesty provided by Christ and admit to each and every fault we own.

Completing the Process of Honesty

Now we are truly ready to address our Creator with "who" we really are. While HONESTY was a critical requirement in the 1st Step, now we will come fully alive in this precious virtue and gift from God.

Please note that the process is possible because Christ has brought us to His altar prepared. We already know the outcome. We have already tasted of His salvation. We are no longer crippled by fear and selfish deceit, but see before us the power that brings true and everlasting peace.

In this most precious moment, all of our humanity is alive to the Good News of Jesus and we are fully free to choose His love and salvation. The process of HONESTY is complete!

I depart from many of those who have journeyed before me and continue on this journey today. Here, therefore, you must mark these thoughts as opinion:

> I do not see the need for writing down where I have been hurt by others or the world. Too many times in the BIG BIG BOOK it tells us to rejoice in our sufferings. If I have held these sufferings as resentments then I am wrong and that is the name of that tune.
>
> We need only focus on where we were wrong. Anyone's retaliation to our actions is either their's to deal with (As a fully focused Christian we would have given immediate forgiveness and not even remembered the incident), or a new fault we have taken on by holding this person away from our love through resentment.
>
> Anything less is playing with the work God will do in our lives. Those that seek to find ways for God to heal their little wounds received from others have not accepted the 3rd Step much less understood the process of the 4th Step.

Final Acceptance of One's Own Life

All of my life I felt the confusion and pain of hidden fears. While it is true that even today I continue to hide shortcomings from my fellow man, earlier in my life most of me was hidden. And I was "hidden" from God.

Yes, I am laughing right along with you. We all know that we cannot hide from God. And yet isn't that what denial is? Hiding from reality. Hiding from God.

It is now time for true inner acceptance of our own humanity. It is time to give up the shadows and dark closets and stand revealed before our Creator. We own up to our lives, and we stand before Our Savior in honest reconciliation.

In the long term we are going to build memories of the process we will go through here and make some very important choices:

✝   Do we ever want to go through an event like this again?

✝   Can we be sure that we do not rebuild another pile of DIS-ease ridden secrets within our lives?

Our answers will come through the following steps of the program, specifically Steps 6 through 10. Now we need to set up the first line of defense - Vigilance. We need to understand that we, alone, cannot protect ourselves from this happening again.

The open kimono principle is our agreement to ourselves that we will no longer deal with the world through subterfuge. We will open our lives so that we have no reason for secrets. (Yes this is a life-long pursuit, but here is where it begins.)

And we will begin to watch for new DIS-ease.

✝ We will be attracted to new areas of DIS-ease. God will point them out to us. We need to be prepared to identify them and mark them as "apart from our walk with Christ."

✝ We will find things we missed within our original 4th Step. These will need to be handled promptly and thoroughly. We are truly given a wonderful gift from our Lord when we approach the 4th Step. He gives us only what we can handle. So we find over time that areas of our lives surface and we need to deal with them. It is God showing us the Creator's wonderful Power and Love and Care.

Through both of these events we can use the process of the 4th Step or the process of the 10th Step to clear the path for the Lord's healing and continued relationship with us. This will be the continuation of the process in God's time, not ours.

The Discipline

There are many ways to go through this process of the 4th Step. Here are the basic ingredients essential to successful fulfillment of this part of the journey:

1. Third Step Prayer
2. Pencil (Pen)
3. Paper
4. Private place to work
5. Secure place to keep documents

Wherever we are on our journey with the Lord, a fearless moral inventory is not something to take lightly. I have in the past shared with open groups of individuals many of the things that have happened in my life and were part of my 4th Step. This does not mean that at the time of the step I should have been able to do the same or even that public confession would even be right! On the contrary, the 4th Step is specifically set up to be private and personal and individual. If we are not fully assured of complete privacy in this event then our very humanness will work against the process. It is said to be impossible for one to dream ones own death. Like this human control point, we cannot fully open ourselves when there is chance for discovery or ridicule.

It is most important to understand that this is for us and us alone. It does not say anything about sharing in the 4th step. It is not proper to do so. It is not right to have this in mind. This is the basic reason for the splitting of the 4th and 5th Steps. The founders knew that, while God can do anything, humans need to take one step at a time.

I have shared the wonderfully debilitating fear I received at the moment I picked up the pen and sat in front of that blank piece of paper. I could not believe that someone could one moment be so in love with the Lord and the next moment totally deny His caring protection. (Silly me! Maybe they should have named me Peter?) Yes, there is a real fear in the process, and yes, we will feel its effects. No, we do not have to give in. That is what fearless is. Accepting the fear as real but moving through it. *The best way I know to move through the fear is to place myself in the arms of my Lord. Therefore I entreat you to begin by writing the 3rd Step Prayer on the top of page one.* From there you and your loving Savior will work to open the soul and relieve the pressures of sin and selfishness.

Format and style will vary based upon your life and comfort. Remember these things to help you:

✟ We are going to be thorough in this process and we will not leave stones unturned. GOD will give us 100% of what needs to be on this paper! God will show us all that needs to be put down so that we can be relieved of the bondage of self.

✟ The BIG BOOK holds a very valid format to use but there are many more to choose from. Be comfortable and be creative.

✟ The only wrong way is to lie to ourselves. Put it all down. You will marvel at the results of your efforts.

The Fifth Step Process

```
┌─────────────────────────────────────────────────┐
│                    STEP #5                        │
├─────────────────────────────────────────────────┤
│ Admitted to God, to ourselves, and to another     │
│ human being the exact nature of our wrongs.       │
│                                                   │
│                 INTEGRITY                         │
├──────────────────────┬──────────────────────────┤
│      BIG BOOK         │          BIBLE            │
├──────────────────────┼──────────────────────────┤
│ Chapter 5 - How it   │ James          5: 16      │
│ Works                │ Proverbs      28: 13      │
├──────────────────────┴──────────────────────────┤
│ Therefore, confess your sins to one another and   │
│ pray for one another, that you may be healed.     │
│ The fervent prayer of a righteous person is very  │
│ powerful.                                         │
│                                      James 5: 16  │
└─────────────────────────────────────────────────┘
```

If we have dedicated ourselves to this "new path with Christ" we will see this step as a natural progression of our spiritual growth. There will be no other step that will bring more fear and emotion. There will be few experiences that will have such a lasting effect.

Hold yourself close to the Lord and follow those who have gone before you. We are truly not unique. In fact, we are so similiar, if anonymous results of Step 4 could be shuffled and passed around you would swear you received your own.

Preparation

We talked about the need for a sponsor. Here we will see an appropriate use for this new type of friend. In sharing our 5th Step, as is identified in the Big Book, there is no need to use our sponsor. I will again share my opinion.

> If we are truly set on making a real journey into areas unknown to us we will be sure to use a guide. Then it seems quite realistic that this guide should have all the information available to help us on this journey. Simply being one who has walked the path in the past will not fulfill all of the opportunities for us. We need to help these guides see where it is God would like us to change. Hence my reason for sharing the 5th Step with your sponsor.

> Now this should lead one to confirm within their own mind that a sponsor should be someone they can trust, someone who understands the 12 Steps (The question I use in selecting a sponsor is "Do you have and use the 12 Steps in your life?") and can be there for the rest of their journey.

> A Spiritual Advisor is, in my opinion, synonymous with sponsor. The only thing that could be missing in this person is a knowledge of the 12 Steps, and I feel sure that they would be more than willing to take the time to learn if asked.

The most important part of this discussion is that the person you choose to share your 5th Step with is available to work by your side through the remaining steps of the program. In other words, a person who is prepared to support you during your journey.

Setting Our Personal Goals

We will set long term goals for this part of the journey. I find it very helpful to have the kingdom of Christ here on earth in focus as we look at this step. I want us to reach out and grasp the hand of Our Savior truly seeking His everlasting forgiveness and comfort.

Here are the goals I suggest for this part of the process:

> Long Term:
> 1. The Opening of Our Own Arms
> 2. Seeing Beyond the Ashes
> 3. Knowing the Price of Peace

The Opening of Our Own Arms

So many times in our lives and in all of the wonderful readings and works about Our Lord we hear and see His open arms. Now we are ready to attempt something which may prove to be more powerful. We are going to open our arms to the Lord.

In the darkness I approached the weeping child. There was no other sound in the room and the pain of this lonely spirit filled my heart with tears. I gently reached out and rested my hand on the little one's shoulder.

There I waited.

Time hurt. I wanted to take the pain away. I sought desperately for a way to break through. There was nothing.

Nothing I could do but wait.
In the stillness of the darkened room, shuddering from its deepest pain, the child turned towards me, opened its arms and rested within my embrace.

You are now home my child and I will hold you till all your tears are gone and your heart is free to feel the peace I have for you.

This is the Jesus I seek in my journey. That is the child I choose to be. Now is the time for us to truly open our arms to the loving embrace of Our Lord. No longer can we stand in the temple praying to an altar. No longer can we exist in a one-sided relationship of worship. No longer can we maintain an impersonal relationship with God and still make this journey meaningful. Now we must act in the most beautiful and, humanly speaking, vulnerable way. We must open ourselves to our Higher Power. Jesus.

Seeing Beyond the Ashes

It is said and professed by those who have walked this way before that, once we truly complete the 5th Step, our past will truly be past and cease to haunt us. I wondered how this could be true? How could this be done when I had suffered with my past for so many years? My guess was that some mystical, unexplainable, "religious" event was going to happen and my past would disappear. Oh! How wonderfully naive I was!

No, again I must warn those looking for smoke and mirrors, this will not prove to be the mystical event. What we need to do now is to see beyond the ashes of our past. We must learn the tools of true human Christianity and see how our past will become the true cornerstone for our spiritually enriched future.
Listen to these key promises in the Big Book:

> *We will not regret the past nor wish to shut the door on it.*

and

> *No matter how far down the scale we have gone, we will see how our experience can benefit others.*

These are not mystical chants of vague rites that magically remove pain and regret. These are the essence of our completeness with Christ as HUMAN CHRISTIANS accepted fully by a Loving and Living Savior!

When we do see through the ashes we see Christ, in all His glory, in all His special and personal Love walking with us in true and lasting reality.

There is no better way to be in this world and there is no greater and truer love than that which Christ holds out to us today.

Knowing the Price of Peace

Finally, we need to see the price of peace. If there is anything we need to learn from this portion of the journey it is that a price will be paid for our happiness. Not in the sense of punishment but in the call to community. For the first time we will be reaching out, not to take love as we so desperately needed in the beginning of this journey, but to share love and to show others the way to the loving arms of Christ.

The price of peace is like the lake that cannot live unless it has a stream flowing out, like a flower that must find a way to spread its pollen in order to live again. We must become a sharing part of the kingdom.

It is at this stage within the 12 Step program that we are said to be truly part of the program. Mostly this statement talks about the dramatic effort we have undertaken in sharing our fourth Step with our sponsor. I think more than this, at least on this spiritual journey, we are closer to the life of Christ than we have been in the past and we are actively taking our place in His kingdom.

Welcome and rejoice in the beauty of the kingdom of Our Lord!

The Discipline

To set rules now would be very pompous of me. There are just a few guidelines and some events from my past that may prove beneficial for your journey.

1. Make sure you set aside enough time for this event. I feel very comfortable allowing an evening for the people I sponsor when we approach this step. It will normally take a good couple of hours to read and pray and discuss the 4th Step. Further, most sponsors will take a few moments to set the stage for the next steps coming up as the 5th leads so nicely into the following events on the journey.

2. Make sure you have the privacy you need. Children and spouses will have your love the rest of their lives. They need you to have the freedom of private time now. It may even be recommended that you take this step away from home so as to assure your peace and quiet.

3. REMEMBER to begin by bringing Christ into your fellowship.

4.   I was taught this when I took my 5th Step. I pass it on for you to use as you see fit.

As the Step states:
✞ Admit to God
✞ Admit to ourselves
✞ Admit to another human being
I had the task, opportunity, requirement to read my 4th Step three times. Do this and I promise that you will know what you have gone through.

5.   Lastly remember the 3rd Step Prayer. If you are already in His arms what is there to fear?

The Sixth Steps Process

STEP #6

Were entirely ready to have God remove all these defects of character.

WILLINGNESS

BIG BOOK	BIBLE	
Humility 12-13, 63	Matthew	Ch. 5, 6 & 7
	Psalm	139
Spiritual Progress	James	4: 1-12
rather than Spiritual	Isaiah	45: 8-10
Perfection 60	1 Peter	5: 5-11

Enter through the narrow gate; for the gate is wide and the road broad that leads to destruction, and those who enter through it are many. How narrow the gate and constricted the road that leads to life. And those who find it are few.
Matthew 7: 13-14

Our journey is now one of continuing growth in the loving arms of Christ. And now, *"Entering the desert,"* we will find how He will work in our life to make us wonderful in His eyes.

The overall message of the 6th Step is the preparation for Christ's work within us. This needs to be understood up front so as not to confuse this part of the process with covering up or showing new masks to the world. This part of the process and the whole journey is based upon the Christ Power we seek to bring our inner spirit in line. In this effort we find wholeness in Christ. We want to build a new "us" that is real and truly pleasing to Christ. Not build facades of goodness to fool others. Therefore the first and most important part of this preparation step is to focus on who will transform us.

During this transformation we may seem to be attempting sainthood. This would certainly lead us very far astray and create a need for a false god to prove our sainthood. We may even need to create a new religion to accept our constant failings as appropriate to sainthood. This is not where we want to be led in this part of the journey.

To understand both our responsibility and that of Christ in this part of the process will empower us and fill us with the proper pathway of true Christianity. This is the key we seek here in the beginning Step of the Desert, to bring ourselves in line with God's grace through Jesus Christ. This is not perfection but direction and acceptance of who we really are in Christ's kingdom.

We will separate the workings of Step 6 from Step 7. This is done to allow the power of each step to be seen, felt and built into our spiritual lives. These two steps form the basis of the "desert journey" and in the overall process blend together like 4 and 5 or 8 and 9. The separation here will be our choice of willingness in the 6th Step and our acceptance of Christ's healing in the 7th Step as a result of our choice.

Preparation

Our preparation for this step is found in two main areas.

First, in the 3rd Step Prayer we have turned ourselves over to His care. We need to remain in this wonderfully compliant position throughout this part of the journey. We need to remain the "child" in His arms seeking only His solace and protection. This is where the attitude of true spiritual growth can become meaningfully effective in our lives.

Second, we have we gone far in uncovering our inner wounds in the frightfully powerful 5th Step. It is said that those who dare to complete this Step are well on their way in spiritual growth.

To let all this wonderful and humbling work go to waste by sitting on the 5th Step would be the worst of tragedies. To not use the gift of the 3rd Step decision would only serve to confuse the process and the work we need to do.

Setting Our Personal Goals

The following goals will enable us to maintain good short and long term disciplines while working this step. These are presented as guidance and measurement tools to our progress.

Short Term:
1. Opening the Heart and Mind
2. Willingness of the Spirit
3. Walking Beyond the Fear

Long Term:
1. Opening the Channel of Cleansing
2. Maintaining Focus on Christ's Work Within Us

We will approach each of these as we think through the process and set our efforts in place. These goals will blend with many of the goals we have set before and enhance those we will set in future steps. For this time, we want to hold them isolated and concentrate on the beauty of the 6th Step process. We want to fully realize their potential in our lives so we can understand what Christ has in store for us in the gift of the 6th Step.

Opening our Heart and Mind to Christ

As with each of the steps prior to this one, we have had to center ourselves, as best we could, in Christ and in His kingdom. Our specific goal here should be one of centering "through the mind, and including the heart." In this we mean to bring ourselves in front of Christ willingly and with "aforethought." Willing ourselves into His presence with knowledge of our actions. We are beyond the child-like emotional invitation and now we need to take up our responsibility to Christ in an adult, knowing way. The heart needs to follow in this process seeking to feel the wonderful healing works of Christ in the process so as to keep us on the path. There will be grave and dire reasons for leaving the path during this process and the heart must be strong and focused on Christ's love for us.

Willingness of the Spirit

We have, to this point in the program, "watched" the spirit grow in us and felt it fill with Christ's love. Now we need to take a more direct involvement with our spirit. It is true that our ultimate goal is to become "One in Spirit with Christ" but this will not happen if we do not take "ownership" of our spirit and prepare it to be joined with Christ in love. We are looking at the very center of our spiritual goal and the ultimate gift of God to His chosen. Here is where our freedom becomes paramount to us and our process. We are now beginning the first few tentative efforts to prepare our spirit for intimate union with Christ.

Walking Beyond the Fear

We have already addressed fear before and there will continue to be opportunities. We will never, in our human existence, move beyond fear. In this part of the process we need to prepare ourselves for this fear and become ready to deal with it. We need to be prepared for one of the main character defects and shortcoming in the nature of man. We are going to allow change, and this is truly against our very nature. We are going to invite change into our lives and attempt to rejoice in its very existence. We are going to accept change as the gift and grace of Christ in our lives throughout our whole being.

Change, the demon we ran from in our DIS-ease. Change, the frightful beast we cowered away from in our dark tunnel of life without Christ. Change, the one thing we cannot control around us and do not want to allow within us. We are going to see and taste and touch the fear of change and walk beyond it into His loving arms.

Opening the Channel of Cleansing

We can certainly remember the DIS-ease, and the work effort expended in the previous five steps. This goal directly relates to the solution of this effort and pain. If we are truly ready to enter into the joy and peace of Christ's kingdom, we will need to maintain our spiritual openness to His grace and love.

It would be so nice and wonderful to spout out magical antidotes for pain and pretend that God will do it for you. But each of us knows deep down this is not relationship. Each of us has taken the different "less traveled" path and we realize that the fullness of love is in freely given service to another.

Here we seek relationship with Christ and we open ourselves to His giving. Here we allow our vulnerability to be our gift to His healing graces, no longer holding back to see what we will get, no longer waiting till He is proven and we know what will happen to us and our life.

This openness requires the deepest challenge of our lives. We have agreed that Christ can and will heal us and care for us. We now need to acknowledge our *Willingness* to allow this healing. When we walk down this new road we do not know where it will lead. We take on a certain trust. Here in our spiritual journey we need to take on the trust we will offer to Christ in His work within us. To give less is to deny Him. To try to continue without this part of the process is to live in a confused and frustrated spiritual anomaly. We know we love Him and want Him - We just don't do it.

In opening a channel, we allow Christ to point to the character defects He wants us to work on. Key points:

✝ He will let us know what to work on.
✝ He will let us know when to work.

Maintaining Focus on Christ's Work Within Us

Our final goal is to set in place the spiritual discipline we will need to continue this part of the process. Our sweet and loving guardian will not give us more than we can handle in one day. He will never leave us and will never force us to leave Him. (Read again the wonderful words of the poem "Footsteps".) With this reliance on His mercy and love we approach the discipline of this Step which is to prepare for Him to change us.

We will find as our spiritual journey continues, He will bring to the surface more that we need to become willing to let Him heal and more for us to clean out so that our intimate relationship can grow and blossom. This is where our part of the work will be. We will need to build a daily discipline to look at and resolve the changes in our lives He brings up to us.

Like many of the steps to come, this goal blends with the detailed work of the past steps and links us to the work in the succeeding steps. Here we set our spiritual lives focused on His work not on what we want done. We drop the pretense of knowing what we want and let Him give us what we need.

More specifically, we need to find a way in our personal lives to foster a means for allowing His work to continue. We will find over time an uneasiness within our being and we will need to reinstate the process of the 6th Step in answer to Christ's call to us. This is where He will renew His life giving work within us and how He will find ways to expand our intimate union.

The Discipline

The following is a method or process for bringing out the fullness of the step in our spiritual journey. It needs to be accepted as one man's experience and with the knowledge that Christ will be the final arbiter in what we will need to do to come to Him. Hopefully you will find these words helpful in building a personal understanding of the step and the ways it can be made real in your spiritual life.

Prepare the Way for the Lord

Of all the steps, this 6th Step is focused directly on preparation. It is here that most of the work will need to be done in our being. It is here that the principle of WILLINGNESS will come alive and fill our life with His wonderful work.

In the beginning of this step we need to allow time to come to understand the nature of the process. We have done much in the last five steps and now we begin to delve into ourselves at a deeper level, and begin to allow Christ into the innermost regions of our soul. This is not something to be taken lightly or without preparation. We need to become able and "willing" to allow this work.

John the Baptist walked the desert for years in preparation for his ministry to the Lord, his one great event in spiritual history on the Jordan. He did not take his preparation lightly. He did not allow his response to God's calling to be an abrupt decision without thought and prayer and guidance. He took the time to understand and see the hand of God in the work before him prior to taking action.

Jesus Himself showed us the need for preparation. He, in His humanness, went out into the desert and brought His being into preparedness for the mission the Creator had for Him. Even our all loving and all powerful Redeemer chose preparedness for the process of His spiritual growth.

So, too, we must become ready for our mission with Christ. This is probably a good way for us to look at this step. We are preparing for the mission Christ has for us. We are choosing to be made ready for the journey on the "narrower pathway of spiritual growth."

The Altar of Love

It is here that we see the ultimate destination of this journey in spirituality and where we recognize Step 6 for what it is, unconditional love to be given to Christ in intimate union. Here in Step 6 we prepare for this union. Here we make ready the way of the Lord in our spiritual lives. Here we take the road less traveled. Here we allow Christ into the depths of our being, fulfilling the greatest expectations of His will for us.

It remains a wonderful mystery how we can see such fear and trepidation in the action of the 4th and 5th Steps but lightly brush over the commitment of the 6th and 7th Steps. Our humanness reacts to the shame of our less than perfect lives and yet we still hold on to this imperfection in light of Christ and His perfect way.

We have come to the altar, dressed in the new clothing of honest repentance and full of His wonderful forgiveness. What will be our response to this ultimate calling of union with the Lord?

The Disciplines of Love

Here is the essence of the work for this part of our journey. We need to identify in our mind, heart and soul the choice of our new life with Christ. We will, in the next step, identify the actions we will take to the stimulus of life and now we must commit ourselves to this new path. Remember always that we are the clay and He is the potter. We are the vessel and He will fill us.

In our work we need to address two major topics; where is our spiritual center and how high will we place this within our life. This is not rhetoric but reality. It is not the time to play with pretty words and quaint phrases of love. It is not the time to romanticize love. We need to address something very real in our lives. How much will we love Christ? There is no softer, easier way to approach Step 6. There needs to be an open, honest acceptance of the new life with Christ and a newly formed attitude as to how we will live within this new life of love and service.

We need to keep the focus of the program and where we are in constant sight as we make this choice. We are not the ones who will do the changing within our lives. *Our responsibility is to be ready for Christ to work within us.* Here is where the choice for love is to be made. Here is where our work in the 6th Step is to be focused. Here is where our growth will find new heights if we accept the challenge of Christ and follow Him.

Lastly, we need to set an attitude of unconditional love. Again, focused on our part in the process we need to choose to react to the world *"as we believe Christ would want us to react."* This is the center of the step and the area we need to realize and instill in our daily lives.

Our actions from this point on will be centered on "self-less" and "Christ-like" actions and not on the selfish actions of the past. We will now see our defects and shortcomings as opportunities to live Christ's life more fully and our attitude will be to choose Christ above the world.

Here is the normal stumbling block for many on this journey, including myself. I felt so ready and yet so worn out from the struggle of being good. What I have come to realize is that I was trying to be God. The 6th Step helps us realize that God wants, can and will fill our lives with spiritual growth and joy. He will make the challenges of leading a Christ-like life fulfilling and not a drain on the human existence. Without this "knowledge/feeling/belief" we will fail to stand up to the pressure of the 6th and subsequent Steps. We will wander in the desert alone and still afraid. We will know Christ but sadly miss His loving strength and peace.

There is no one among us who does not want to be good and holy and just. We need to learn to allow this to happen in the most perfect of ways. We need to allow Christ to fulfill us. Then, in the gentleness of His loving power, He will shape us in the true beauty of His likeness.

> You were dead in your transgressions and sins in which you once lived following the age of this world, following the ruler of the power of the air, the spirit that is now at work in the disobedient. All of us once lived among them in the desires of our

flesh, following the wishes of the flesh and the impulses, and we were by nature children of wrath, like the rest. But God, who is rich in mercy, because of the great love He had for us, even when we were dead in our transgressions, brought us to life with Christ (by grace you have been saved), raised us up with Him, and seated us with Him in the heavens in Christ Jesus, that in the ages to come He might show the immeasurable riches of His grace and kindness to us in Christ Jesus. For by grace you have been saved through faith, and this is not from you; it is a gift of God; it is not from works, so no one can boast. For we are His handiwork, created in Christ Jesus for the good works that God has prepared in advance, that we should live in them.

Ephesians 2: 1-10

We take this step with gladness in our hearts and wonderful anticipation in our souls. Now we have the choice to choose Christ. This is the attitude instilled by the 6th Step and the wonderful joy of its completion. We will be in His arms not out of need as in the first three steps but out of deep desire and choice. We are now ready. We are now willing. We are now freely part of the intimate relationship with Christ.

The Seventh Step Process

STEP #7

Humbly asked Him to remove our shortcomings

HUMILITY

BIG BOOK	BIBLE	
Humility 12-13, 63	John	3: 3- 6
	Psalm	51
	Luke	18: 9-14

"But the tax collector stood off at a distance and would not even raise his eyes to heaven but beat his breast and prayed, 'O God, be merciful to me a sinner.'..."

Luke 18: 13

It is here where our journey will realize the essence of Christ's power. It is here where we will act on this power and become truly one of Christ's disciples. The desert journey is one of inner change and this Step is the ultimate response to this change.

Hold out your life as a spiritual gift to the Lord and you will find His kingdom here on earth.

Preparation

Our preparation for this Step is one of finalization of the 6th Step. We cannot do anything but await the workings of the Lord in our lives. We have already done what it is we need to do.

However, many of us need to and should begin a ritual of being ready. Like any relationship, there is a need for constant refreshment of our vow. This is what we see in the essence of the "7th Step Prayer":

> *"My Creator, I am now willing that You should have all of me, good and bad. I pray that You should remove from me every single defect of character which stands in the way of my usefulness to You and my fellows. Grant me strength, as I go out from here, to do Your bidding.*
>
> *Amen.*

This simple prayer begins the day Christ focuses us on His kingdom and His work. This is the best and most direct way to prepare for this Step, both in the beginning of its use and daily throughout our journey with Christ.

Setting Our Personal Goals

The following goals meet the long and short term objectives of our journey. These two goals will enable us to keep focused on the 7th Step and receive the benefits of Christ's grace through this portion of the process:

> Short and Long Term:
> 1. Keeping in love with Christ
> 2. Accepting the doubt and going forward

We need to maintain and confirm our intimate relationship with Christ for this part of the journey. Here we can identify with the feelings and attitudes necessary for maintaining the relationship and allowing our humanness to work through this Step.

Keeping in Love with Christ

When we reach out to someone in intimate relationship we can easily see how little quirks of our personality can be left behind to improve and enjoy the relationship. I really don't mind picking up my socks when I realize it helps to comfort my wife. I can do dishes when I see that it brings pleasure to my spouse. It is this very point we want to instill into our spiritual life.

I always loved the game of Kris Kringle, doing something special for another without them knowing it. It gave me the ability to ACT ON MY LOVE for them freely. It is this form of love and free giving that we need to build within our spiritual tool bag. This is the sense of freedom and love we want to offer to Christ in this Step, giving of ourselves for the joy of it, giving freely with a sense of gladness.

Keeping this type of love in our daily lives is the attitude of renewed commitment to the gift we have given to Christ. It is our daily choice to remain in the arms of the Lord. It is our right and privilege to be one with the Lord forsaking self.

This attitude will bring us to the starting point of the Step. God will use this attitude to sharpen and beautify our very nature for His work. The attitude is one of acceptance of His work in us and the continued vow of love.

Accepting the Doubt and Going Forward

What good is commitment if it is never tested.

This may NOT be what we expected to hear. We look at James 2: 14-26 to see the need for working with the Lord as He builds us in His image. Keeping in love is very good and very important but we must be prepared to let go of the defects He points out to us. We must allow the change. We must do what He requests of us. We must walk through the doubt and fear of change when and as He requests. This is our commitment in the 7th Step and the essence of the test of our growing spiritual life.

> A man stood before St. Peter and asked why he had died in the flood. "I was good and always loved the Lord. I stood on my roof during the flood and professed to everyone that My Lord would save me! Why didn't you answer my prayers?"
>
> Peter frowned and said, "We sent you two boats and a helicopter, what more did you expect."

In His wonderful gift of life He has given us free will so we do have the choice to serve Him and here in the 7th Step we make that choice. It is time to begin to row the boat. He will steer but we need to row if we expect to get to the other side.

Of all the stories, those where one sacrifices their desires for another hits home and hits deep within my being. Listen to the words Jesus Himself used:

> "This is my commandment: Love one another as I love you. No one has greater love than this, to lay down one's life for one's friends.
>
> 1 John 15: 12-13

Therefore, the goal of acceptance is not the negative goal of suffering but the beautifully freeing goal of giving true love. Of all the Steps to this point, the 7th Step reaches deepest into the true meaning of love. We have had relationship and acceptance of others' help. Now we see our personal gift of giving within our relationship with Christ.

The Discipline

The discipline for this step is easy to talk about but difficult to explain and document. Each of us will be approached by Christ differently. Changes in our life will be brought about on His schedule and by His methods. We can do three things to keep ourselves working this step properly:

1. Know the signs of needed change
2. Document and journal changes being worked on
3. Remember to smile

Know the Signs of Needed Change

Knowing the signs should be very evident from the past six steps. We know the powerful reactions of disease or the irksome fret of DIS-ease in our spiritual life. These same feelings (smaller but still present) will be our alarm and our invitation to act in love to Christ's call.

Here is a point on progress and perfection.
It is not ours to choose what needs to be corrected or when. He has accepted this part of the relationship. We do need to progress in our relationship and therefore in our growth and development. That is what will happen through the workings and dedication of the 7th Step.

Document and Journal Changes Being Worked On

This effort, or better yet advice, follows the actions we learned in the 4th Step. What we write down becomes clearer and impossible to bury in our sub-conscious. We can not deny what we put to paper and see for ourselves.

Beyond this there is the benefit of growth through repetition of learned and valid actions from past growth. Here we can see where and how we have grown through Christ's workings and see how to put this effort to use on the next challenge He presents to us.

Remember to Smile

This may be the most important piece of advise. This is a love relationship and all work done here is a gift not a task. We need to keep our sense of humor available so that we do not end up wearing our cross as an afflicted martyr for our own cause. We must understand that while change is work, it is not the end of the world and not a suffering or punishment. Remembering to smile will keep us in the spirit of change, and in the spirit of the gift of the 7th Step that we offer to Christ.

In Closing

This step and the desert it comes from seems difficult to most who approach the journey and impossible for those outside the path. It truly is our gift to Christ. It is the our first real action within His kingdom by our own choice and it is one of the most wonderful presents we can offer. Find this gift and offer it to Him with your love. You will touch the essence of happiness and joy. You will know that this relationship is worth the work and the journey.

Look back and see the progress. Through the 6th and 7th Steps we have truly formed a new "us" to be given to Christ in love. We have prepared and presented to Christ the person we always wanted to be for Him. As the old saying goes - "We've come a long way."

The Eighth Step Process

STEP #8

Made a list of all persons we had harmed, and became willing to make amends to them all.

BROTHERLY LOVE

BIG BOOK	BIBLE	
Willingness 12-13, 26, 46, 47, 53, 57, 60, 69, 70, 76, 79, 93, 118, 124, 152, 153, 158, 159, 162	Matthew	7: 3 - 5
	Roman	14: 9-12

Let love be sincere; hate what is evil, hold on to what is good; love one another with mutual affection; anticipate one another in showing honor. Do not grow slack in zeal, be fervent in spirit, serve the Lord. Rejoice in hope, endure in affliction, persevere in prayer. Contribute to the needs of the holy ones, exercise hospitality. Bless those who persecute [you], bless and do not curse them. Rejoice with those who rejoice, weep with those who weep. Have the same regard for one another; do not be haughty but associate with the lowly; do not be wise in your own estimation. Do not repay anyone evil for evil; be concerned for what is noble in the sight of all. If possible, on your part, live at peace with all. Beloved, do not look for revenge, but leave room for wrath; for it is written, "Vengeance is mine, I will repay, says the Lord." Rather, "if your enemy is hungry, feed him; if he is thirsty, give him something to drink; for by so doing you will heap burning coals upon his head." Do not be conquered by evil but conquer evil with good.

Romans 14: 9 - 21

In the fullness of time, Jesus will show us how all of this world fits together in His kingdom. Now we need to set ourselves truly in His presence and begin to do His work His way! We have come to the time of working in His vineyard and we will work in a new way and a new light.

Preparation

This Step will be one of preparation. As such it always seems to get over with quickly. In fact the basic physical effort is really done in the 4th and 5th Steps. However, we do have a good deal of work to do in the mental and spiritual realms of our life for the 8th Step. We need to prepare ourselves to allow Christ to work through us.

Many have sought to understand the power of Our Savior. Now we will see His working within our lives and we will KNOW HIS POWER. There will indeed be significant effort and personal commitment to working this step.

The 8th and 9th Steps are to rebuild bridges between relationships that have been broken or left in disrepair. This rebuilding is the fullness of community within our church and needs to be handled with diligence and great care. What we do in the next two Steps will preview how the rest of our journey will progress and how close we will be able to get to Our Lord.

Setting Our Personal Goals

Our goals will be both short term and long term in order to set up a road-map of how Jesus will work in our lives to bring us to the fullness of His grace.

> Short Term:
> 1. Opening to the Seventh Step Commitment
> 2. Allowing God to Override Our Feelings
>
> Long Term:
> 1. Understanding True Discipleship
> 2. Living Brotherly Love

Each of these goals are something we have always wanted within our lives. They have always seemed to be the key actions of living a peace filled life. Yet somehow they have not been easy to attain. In Romans we see the pleading for consistency of love within the community with the cornerstone of love to all.

Opening to the 7th Step Commitment

Look back within our own journey to the process of the 2nd Step. There we set the short term goals of "seeking, finding and confirming" Christ in our lives. Now we will focus more sharply on the work that God puts in front of us this day.

In the 7th Step Prayer we dedicated ourselves, both good and bad, to His will. Now we need to actually begin this very process. We are now a gift to Christ! How can we do anything but His will and do it in a way pleasing to Him? How can we continue to put our human barriers in front of the path He will take us on?

This process of opening is the focal point we will establish within ourselves to make sure we are on the path of Christ. Note, we are not looking around us for the path. Notice that we did not blindly accept the path of our sponsor or some other leader. Notice the beautiful growth we have already had from this wonderful program. We are standing on our own, facing our Creator, taking up the "cross" of our journey and becoming whole in our personal relationship with Christ.

We have fully chosen this life. Now we are ready to begin to act.

Many will ask, "why not just run out and make the amends?" While there are some pragmatic reasons, not the least of which is that we still need some guidance, the most important is that in this new life with Christ "WE DON'T - HE DOES." And so we prepare. We get ready for His workings in our life and allow Him to guide and direct this process of building bridges.

Allowing God to Override Our Feelings

Made a list of all persons we had harmed.....

But he was the one that started it!

She always liked the others better. She always treated me as if I was second rate. Why should I apologize to her? She is the one who pulled away and ignored me.

I just cannot face her. There is just too much pain and guilt. I cannot!

Hell! They don't even know what I did. Why open up a can of worms?

.... and became willing to make amends to them all.

Our very life is challenged in this action of our new faith life. We are no longer alone in our world and we need to understand and continually commit to our new way of life. It would be best to call our new life a discipline, *or as Christ put it, a discipleship.* And so we reach out into our new spirituality and take on the life of Christ.

In this 8th Step we stand before God and prepare for His work. Our only job is to list and to pray. The list is easy, as can be seen from the examples above and the thoughts already floating around in our heads. The willingness is tough. "The spirit is willing but the flesh is weak..." (Matthew 26:41).

Therefore, our goal in this 8th Step is to have Christ help us build up the willingness to continue and complete this portion of the journey. Pray for the willingness. We once saw how wonderfully He took care of us as individuals. How much more can we expect from Him as He cares for us among His favored flock? Will He not continue in His divine wisdom and love to make our life pleasing to Him and fill us with beauty and wonderful opportunities for love? Will He not remain our Higher Power and hold us in the palm of His hand?

For our sake and the sake of all who will love us knock on this door and become willing.

Understanding True Discipleship

Now we can look into the future a little and see the message of true discipleship within our very lives. Can we remember the time Jesus girded Himself and knelt to wash the feet of the apostles? Look now at the work in front of us. Have we not been called to true discipleship? Is this the true cross we are supposed to carry in our lives with Christ?

We have laid down the burdens built from our fear, our humanness and our guilt. We have taken up a new cross and a new life. Here we stand on the threshold of our new journey with Christ and we have been shown the essence of our true task.

> *"I give you a new commandment: love one another. As I have loved you, so you also should love one another. This is how all will know that you are my disciples, if you have love for one another."*
>
> *John 13: 34-35*

Ours is not to correct, to judge, to change. Ours is to love. These simple, direct, beautiful, words of Our Savior are the focal point of this 8th Step and the entire program of the 12 Steps to Spirituality. We have found the source, the wellspring for our power, now we have found the action and the flow of the river we will receive from His true love. That is, to love one another in return for His gifts to us.

With this we can surely see the essence of the 8th Step preparation. We should be able to almost instantly feel the reason behind not worrying about self but looking only at how we can aid another. We can see His commandment and the means to accomplish His will.

Living Brotherly Love

This is the link to the 9th Step. It is the action we take as Christ guides us to do His will. It is that moment in time when we again renew our love for Christ and submit to His work as servant and disciple. Brotherly Love is the essence of Christ's spiritual message. He has given us the GIFT of Brotherly Love so that we could come to Him.

We need to maintain this love in our daily journey with Christ so that we are assured of the very best relationship with Christ.

Someone once told me that if each Christian reached out to five individuals with love it would be literally impossible for war and strife. If we could just touch five people and show them the beauty of the Lord, His kingdom could be complete.

Please receive the message here. In this the 8th Step we as humans need to pray for the willingness to reach out to those we love already. Can we see how living true brotherly love will take us far beyond this world that holds us in fear? Can we see how truly easy it can be to live fully in the Kingdom of God? Can we reach into eternity and touch the hand of Our Lord? The answer, found by many before us, and assured by the Man from Galilee is YES.

The Discipline

We have prepared so much there seems little to do in the discipline. I love the following "LIST" and offer it to you for your beginnings.

NOW	LATER
MAYBE	NEVER

PLACE THE NAMES OF THOSE WHOM YOU CANNOT MAKE AMENDS TO IN THE NEVER BOX, THOSE YOU ARE UNSURE OF IN THE MAYBE BOX, THOSE WHOM YOU WANT TO IN THE LATER BOX, AND THOSE THAT YOU ARE WILLING TO IN THE BOX MARKED NOW.

AS YOU MAKE AMENDS TO THOSE IN THE NOW, THE LATERS BECOME NOW, WHILE THE MAYBES BECOME LATERS, AND THOSE WHOM YOU HAVE SAID NEVER TO MOVE UP IN YOUR HEART UNTIL CHRIST GIFTS YOU WITH THE PRESENT OF NOW.

WHEN IN DOUBT - ASK YOUR SPONSOR.

The List

We need to bring forward, from our 4th and 5th Steps, the individuals who have been armed by our actions. These names are WRITTEN down so that we can keep them within our conscious process of healing. We can then begin the process of asking God for the willingness to make amends.

I digress to opinion.

> Ours is not to list what was done to us. We have been healed and held and loved and cuddled throughout the first seven Steps. We are not the ones who were hurt by our actions. Therefore I find it inconsistent to put our name on this list. In fact I find it goes against the very grain of the program which is a spiritual lesson in self-less-ness. Our pains and sufferings, while real, are not the concern of this Step. We are here to do the will of the one who will send us, and that is Jesus. He has commanded. We obey.

The Big Book and many other sources will show many creative ways to make and maintain this list. Mine was a piece of paper in my wallet. Please feel free to choose a style which suits your needs and desires. Many have included with the list a main reason for having to make the amends. I never felt I would forget, and besides, I always went to my sponsor prior to making an amends. In this way we both confirmed what it was we believed Christ wanted.

I digress to opinion once more.

Whatever the method selected for this effort the key will be the prayer for willingness and the focus on what Christ wants us to do. If there are people whom we do not want to make amends to, make sure they are on the list. Leaving these people off the list has been the downfall of many on this journey. We are loved by God. Each person on earth is loved by God. How can we hold back our love from one of His?

To be given the opportunity to make things right once more, to be able to stand in front of one of Christ's children and present a new and living "self" is the essence of this part of the process. While we may see both fear and guilt standing in our way, pray that we also see the beauty and peace of the results Christ will attain for us in our endeavors.

The Ninth Step Process

STEP #9
Made direct amends to such people wherever possible, except when to do so would injure them or others.
JUSTICE

BIG BOOK	BIBLE
Chapter 5 - How it Works	Matthew 5: 21-26

You have heard that it was said to your ancestors 'You shall not kill; and whoever kills will be liable to judgement.' But I say to you, whoever is angry with his brother will be liable to judgement, and whoever says to his brother "Raqa" will be answerable to the Sanhedrin, and whoever says 'You fool,' will be liable to the fiery Gehenna. Therefore, if you bring your gift to the altar, and there recall that your brother has anything against you, leave your gift there at the altar, go first and be reconciled with your brother, and then come and offer your gift."

Matthew 5: 21 - 24

Amends. In *Love Story* they said "love is not having to say your sorry". And now a whole generation has found a way to ignore the central theme of true forgiveness. Amends.

Preparation

Amends goes far beyond the act of saying "I'm Sorry." It is the fullness of true love and community life within the kingdom of Christ. Amends benefits me. While others may benefit from the action I take in offering restitution, I am the one who has the true and lasting benefit. I am the one who is reconciled with the Lord by this act of atonement.

I have always believed that amends is not just saying "I'm Sorry." In fact, we will see that, within the context of this 12 Step process, amends will take on a much deeper role. For now we want to prepare for the task ahead and there are three things we need to focus on and remember:

> 1. God's will, not mine be done.
> 2. It is my new life I offer.
> 3. Humiliation is lack of Humility.

This 9th Step is focused on the principle of JUSTICE. We can get very concerned with the outcome of this event if we do not look deeply and allow Christ into our actions. Therefore, the first item to remember is:

God's Will

We need to assure ourselves that we are on God's pathway to recovery and not ours. For many of us we have used "I'm sorry" and "excuse me" to get over those who blocked our path. To walk up to my wife, after years of torment, and say I'm sorry would have been a very interesting situation to say the least.

Maybe we can see now why this part of the journey is so far down in the 12 Steps. We were truly not prepared to make amends much less bring any new hope of relationship in the beginning. What has happened is that we have now rebuilt our lives and ways and can offer something new and better to those we love. We can build new bridges within our own relationships based upon the love of Christ and our new way of life. We are now whole and have something worth while to offer our brother or sister.

This, I believe, is God's will. To stand now in front of our brother or sister, in Christ, and offer ourselves for service and love and forgiveness.

New Life

This leads directly to the central theme of our amends and our second point, offering our new life. Yes, we ask for forgiveness and make restitution for our past mistakes. But most important is that we offer, to those we approach in this Step, a new and changed life based upon service and love through Jesus Christ. This is what will make all the difference. This is what will change the outcome of apology. This is what will create the new bridge of love and service.

Humility vs. Humiliation

Finally there needs to be a new and fully understood attitude for this process to be of benefit to us or anyone else. That is an attitude of true humility based upon the gifts of the Spirit and the life we have been given through Jesus Christ.

If we approach someone and we feel humiliated, then we have not prepared for this part of the process. Yes we will indeed be humbled. In fact, we may be persecuted for the very act of seeking forgiveness and reconciliation. But to be humiliated is to not have stood up to the facts of our past life and normally means we have very little new to offer.

Think of going to apologize for breaking a window with the knowledge that we fully intend to do it again. Can we stand before them in true humility? Can we really seek forgiveness? Or are we still caught up in the DIS-ease of our past life? And if they attack our sincerity, how will we react? Is this not the humiliation we know from our past lives?

Now is the new life in Christ. Now is the change in the process of our being. Now is the time for true humility. Use this as the barometer for our progress. If humiliated, seek to review our own growth and where Christ is in our journey.

Setting Our Personal Goals

Our goals for this 9th Step will all be long term. Yes, there will be many actions in the immediate future but they all will have far reaching effects on our lives and the lives of those we meet on our journey.

> Long Term:
> 1 The Vigilance of Agape Love (Charity)
> 2 The Tender Heart
> 3 Seeking the Lord's Work

The Vigilance of Agape Love (Charity)

The only true relationship with meaning is one that is based upon service to the Lord. If we are truly living this new "self-less" life with Christ, we will want to re-build these relationships not for ourselves but for the service we can do for the Lord in His kingdom. This is certainly not to say that we will see no benefit from these events. To the contrary, we will be building an ever expanding circle of friends and intimate relationships that are all focused in God's world.

And we will be building a smaller list of those, currently unable to accept this pathway of Christ, who are a truly special gift to us. These are the future saints Christ has given to us for our prayers of intercession.

> I have heard it said that I am to "keep my side of the road clean" and the rest is up to them. There is a sadness in this message.

I have heard it said that "If they don't accept Christ then they can go their own way. I will have nothing to do with them." There is a very important misunderstanding of Christ's central message of love in these words.

Without getting off the mark of this 9th Step we need to see how we fit within Christ's kingdom and how our Agape Love needs to be spread over the lives Christ has given to us to share His word with. Anyone who has chosen to only give to those who understand Christ and His ways does not know Christ and needs to truly begin the process of these Steps again.

The Tender Heart

Meditate on the many times Jesus broke through all the traditions and complex social requirements to touch the lives of those in SIN. Think of how many times He focused on doing for the "least of these". Think on His very words, that He came for the SINNERS. Whom did He sit at the table with? Whom did He spend personal time with at the well? Whom did he admonish when there was judgement at hand and stones to be thrown?

There can only be one answer for us at this stage of the process. We need to build and maintain a tender heart. We need to be fortified by true compassion, seeing only Christ in the eyes and heart and soul of the precious gift brought before us to share the relationship of Our Savior.

The Tender Heart is the one who understands the Beatitudes. It is the one who understands the full meaning of the cross. It is:

✝ *the heart who has acknowledged its own failings and can see no one who has failed more to love the Lord;*

✝ *the heart that has known the wonderful forgiveness of the Lord despite all its weakness;*

✝ *the heart that can see into the very soul of those before it and see the spark of Christ at work;*

✝ *the heart that desires to be the arms of Christ for those in need.*

Please see this from the journey you have already accomplished. Please see this as the central theme of the work you will do for the Lord. Please feel the true power of Christ through Agape Love and Service.

Seeking the Lord's Work

Now we can see what we are called to do. The Lord's work for us is to be the new doorway. The opening for those who seek to find Him.

We have been:

✟   cleaned and cared for by the great Physician;

✟   dressed and prepared by the Perfect Teacher;

✟   honed in the fire of honesty and humility;

✟   given the gifts and joys of Christ's Love.

Now we are called to the task. We are called, by intimate invitation, to the wedding feast of Our Savior, Jesus Christ. We have become the chosen ones who will spread the Good News to all who suffer and are in pain. We have become the vessel from which Christ will pour out His Love and Compassion on all those we meet and can touch for Him.

And, no greater love can a one have than to pour out one's life for another. Isn't the Lord's Work the most beautiful of all the promises of this 12 Step Program. Welcome to the journey of the Lord!

The Discipline

Wow! Have we really opened up this much? Have we really come this far? The answer is truly yes.

Our work has brought us back to the world and ready to do the will of the Lord who has sent us. (Now don't get your traditional brains in a tizzy. I am not replacing Jesus.) What we are doing is being what Christ wants us to be. Remember, "They will know you are Christians by your Love." We are now truly, physically, mentally and spiritually Christ's Love. And in the representation of Christ through the dedication of our service we have been formed in His image.

The discipline of this step is very simple:

1. Keep your list of names available.
2. Talk with your sponsor before making amends to a particular person.
3. Invite Christ into the amends before you start.

He will already be there since He will be the one to bring the people in front of you at the right time. Remember how we sought the willingness in the 8th Step. Remember how we let ourselves be cared for in the 3rd and 7th Step prayers. Now we will act on these very principles, "His will not mine be done."

Stand back for a moment and look out at the life before us. We have been given one of the most unique and wonderful gifts known. We have been given a new chance to fully understand Christ's kingdom here on earth and to know our place in it.

Now we are given the first of the public tasks of this new life with Christ. It will be a task we will work on for the rest of our days here on earth. See the beauty and the wonderful joy of this task. We will be able to touch the very lives of those loved by our Creator. We will be the vessel that Christ uses to bring His message of love and forgiveness. We will truly be the servant of the Lord and feel the wonderful joy of the Lord as His children turn to Him for love and safety.

There could be no better chance for real happiness in this or any other world. The Kingdom of God is here and now and we are all a part of His wonderful life of love.

The Tenth Step Process

STEP #10

Continued to take personal inventory and when we were wrong promptly admitted it.

PERSEVERANCE

BIG BOOK	BIBLE	
Humility 12-13, 63	Proverbs	28: 13
	James	3: 13-18
	II Corinthians	13: 5-13
	1 John	1: 5-10

Who among you is wise and understanding? Let him show his works by a good life in the humility that comes from wisdom. But if you have bitter jealousy and selfish ambition in your hearts, do not boast and be false to the truth. Wisdom of this kind does not come down from above but is earthly, unspiritual, demonic. For where jealousy and selfish ambition exist, there is disorder and every foul practice. But the wisdom from above is first of all pure, then peaceable, gentle, compliant, full of mercy and good fruits, without inconsistency or insincerity. And the fruit of righteousness is sown in peace for those who cultivate peace.

James 3: 13-18

This 10th Step will be the step turned to most often throughout our lives and will become the culmination of the previous steps. There are those who see this as the beginning of the breakthrough to our new spiritual self and therefore attach this step to the 11th and 12th Steps. There are those who see this as the finishing touch for the work done from Step 1 through 9 completing the process of bridge building. I enjoy the latter approach. This is the final step in the process of building our relationships with the community we will live in and serve. From here we will move to the higher spiritual plane and make an even deeper contact with our Personal Savior enhancing our life in the process.

This Step is the embodiment of the process of our new life and, followed on a continual basis, will give us the accomplishments and direction we will need throughout our lives.

Preparation

The first time we use our newly cleaned room, our keys and wallet are not haphazardly tossed but placed in the appropriate place on the bureau. This is also the way of a newly cleaned and renewed soul. We are still filled with the wonderful excitement of cleanliness and we want to keep everything "spic n' span." We make the effort to maintain this pristine position with Our Lord and hold on to the wonderful feeling of worth and peace that this cleanliness brings.

It would be a kingdom of perfection if this state could be maintained. It is the promise of eternity we have received from God in heaven through Jesus Christ, but it is not the fact of our world today. No, we will not remain in this state of euphoria. No, we can not expect Christ to keep us out of harms way, since He will not take away our free will. No, we have not found nirvana or our own paradise.

And so we prepare for the reality of the kingdom of God here on earth. We prepare for a series of actions that will keep us in the arms of Christ and help us from going too far astray. We build within our lives a discipline of vigilance and perseverance. We practice and make the 10th Step part of our new spiritual life.

Setting Our Personal Goals

Our goals from here-on-out will be described in one category. Long term would seem to be the best definition, but truly there is no long or short. There is only life today with our Higher Power. Lets just call them "All Time Goals."

> All Time:
> 1. Constancy of Effort
> 2. Creation of Self Discipline
> 3. Dedication to His Life and Way

Constancy of Effort

First we need to take control through constant and continuous surveillance of our life's actions and results. In the 6th and 7th Steps we decided on our new way of life. In the 8th and 9th we presented this new life to our community. Now in the 10th Step we set in motion the actions that will maintain this life and keep us within our new commitment to Christ.

Look once again at the words of the 7th Step. *"My Creator, I am now willing that You should have all of me, good and bad...."* With these words we turned our journey over to Christ as an offering. This journey contains the humbling reality of one's inability to reach perfection. It contains the fact that without Christ we will not survive, much less attain perfection. Now we stand before the new dawn and see the challenge imparted by our choice of this spiritual road. And we see the need to maintain a constant vigilance in order to keep on the path Christ has laid before us.

The simplicity of the 10th Step hides it's power. I have many times used a coffee can and coins to show this power. When there are no coins within the can and you toss one in, you will hear the reverberating sound. But if you allow the can to fill with coins, the next one lands with a dull clink. No alarm, just the same old pain and continued deterioration of the spirit. *This was what our 4th Step was made up of.* This is what we have to guard against. Of all the pains I have gone through in this world, the worst has been the humbling pain of the 4th Step. I do not intend to place myself in that kind of bottom again. Therefore, I choose constancy of effort to control and protect against this horrible outcome.

Creation of Self Discipline

To this point in the program we have been following the lead of logical steps, advice from sponsors, information gleaned from the Big Book, the Big Big Book, and our conscience. Now we will begin a new and more personal process of working within ourselves and using the power we have been given by Christ. We have been disciples. Now it is time to fly and to use our "self-discipline."

Self-discipline is the result of following. It is the outward sign that we have followed, understood, and accepted the teachings of those who have shared with us. It is the final stage in the teaching process and the goal we need to attain to be truly free and able to claim the life Christ has given us.

I have heard that there is a "new tradition" that goes something like this:

> Since we cannot be saved without Christ,
> then He will save us and our efforts have
> no consequence. Therefore it is our right
> in life to live as we wish and Christ's duty
> to save us.

Puppets would be a kind and somewhat thoughtful interpretation for this group of new age thinkers. Creators of a false god would be much more to the point.

Since we have been saved through the love and service and sacrifice of Christ, we must now accept His love and the commission HE GAVE to share this love with others. We have seen through the previous 9 Steps that we cannot love, at least like Christ loves, unless we are open and filled with His Spirit. And we have seen that He will not find room to work within us if we are filled and confused with sin.

Our New Age friends have missed some important facts of our salvation history. We must not loose our way in this world filled with confusion and sin. We must not allow twisted words to keep us from the internal truth we have found within the 12 Step Journey. Keep in mind the process and the logic of staying whole and clean for the Lord's work. Keep in mind the serenity and peace we have found through this journey and we will not be led astray.

We have grown and can now fully rely on the mind and soul and spirit within us. We can see with our mind's eye the truth for our life with Christ. We are now able to be "self-disciplined" and to walk within the world free and confident in our life and our relationship with Our Savior.

Dedication to His Life and Way

Finally, we dedicate ourselves to His life and way. We are now truly and completely a part of His kingdom, standing tall and ready to serve in love and peace. If we have been diligent in our efforts we are already seeing this as a wonderful opportunity rather than a challenging chore or duty. In fact, we are feeling the presence of Christ filling us with strength and determination *prior to our efforts to remain in His arms.*

We have come to a place of true wholeness and peace. We have become fully human in the eyes of our Creator.

Human, can this be what we have sought for all this time? Can humanity, with all its faults and failings, be what He wants of us?

Listen carefully to the following words with our renewed and cleansed heart. Listen deeply with our refreshed and softened soul. Listen quietly with the wisdom of our spirit.

> "Then God said: 'Let us make man in our own image, after our likeness......
> God created man in His image, in the divine image He created him; male and female He created them.....
> And so it happened. God looked at everything He had made, and He found it very good...."
>
> Genesis 1: 26-31

Welcome to the wonderful gift of humanity. Welcome to the reality of God and life itself. Welcome to the kingdom of God here on earth.

In our dedication to this path of spiritual growth we will eventually come full cycle to the completeness of our humanity in the eyes of our loving God. God created us out of Love, gave us free will out of Love, and will stand with us out of Love. Our Creator sent Jesus to bear witness to God's love for us and Jesus sacrificed His life for our humanity.

We now know truly who and what we are. We now see God joyfully inviting us home once more and we have the free will to use the 10th Step process to accept this invitation to love.

The Discipline

I am sharing my experience, strength and hope. This leaves me with a major dilemma to address now and in the next few steps. While I have some words of wisdom passed down to me and experiences that you may find helpful, I am truly only a child in this and the remaining steps. Indeed, these writings have been part of the process of daily growth for me in my own journey.

I ask, therefore, that you gently sift through these words as a friend. Take hold of what you see as gems and gently discard the rest with a prayer for my continuing journey with the Lord.

The following daily routines may prove helpful in your journey:

1. Daily Prayer Focus
2. Journaling
3. Advanced Sponsorship
4. The Knight of the Mirror

Daily Prayer Focus

If there is one place we can each start to practice the principles of this 10th Step it is prayer. Now, while it is true that we will dedicate the next step almost exclusively to this important part of our life, we need to make prayer a daily event that is used to focus our life and our direction.

In the early part of the program, before the steps, we spent time working with sayings that helped us find a direction for our lives. One Day at a Time.... Keep it Simple.... These helped us focus on the new life. Here is a simple prayer taught from the first moments of the program:

God please keep me away from _____
today.

This is prayer at its elemental level. It is good and just and real and, in my opinion, extremely necessary. It is here that we bring our being in line with Christ and His kingdom. It is our outward sign of wanting Him to guide and direct our day.

If after a day we have made it home safe and warm I was taught to pray this:

Thank You.

Make prayer a focus and a focal point of our day. It will grow and expand to meet the needs of the challenges we will face. Prayer will provide the needed direction for our human journey with our Divine Lord and Savior.

Journaling

This, similar to the 4th step process, allows us to put the event that needs correction in black and white. It will give us the needed insight into the dilemma we face and allow us, over time, to see our progress in our spiritual growth.

I have always found this to be a difficult process and only used this form of 10th Step discipline in times of extreme trouble. When used, I have seen the power. I fall short of the constancy that would benefit my life.

Advanced Sponsorship

Sponsorship, to this point, has been to show us the new way of life as identified by the 12 Steps. Now we are ready and may be willing to take this one step further. In sponsorship we can begin a dialogue between "two equal travelers". This is where the sponsor is no longer the teacher but the companion on the journey and the sharing becomes a two way street.

This is the time most who have sponsored look forward to in a continuing relationship. While many encounters will lead to friendship and continued contact, some will evolve to this higher plane of endeavor and become something truly unique. No longer the teacher, the sponsor can share without the caution of minding the child of God. No longer the student, we can begin to form and voice our own understandings and opinions of our faith journey. This is a relationship that is truly alive in Christ and can attain very deep levels of growth and spiritual involvement. This is a sharing of the journey in its deepest human tradition.

The Knight of the Mirror

Always enchanted by the tale of Don Quixote, I see the power of the message formed by the character of the Knight of the Mirrors. Here, to bring the "old man" back into reality, the knight makes him face his own image. In the stark reality of the mirror Don Quixote sees the shaving basin instead of the helmet, a windmill instead of a dragon. He is stricken down by the reality of his life.

We need to follow this example and look within the mirror seeking the truth. No matter how well we would like to hide it in justice and righteous anger and other reasons we must see our actions for what they really are and respond when they are inappropriate.

In closing, I hope you find the "all time goals" of this step within your life. By keeping in touch with ourselves and our spiritual conditioning, we will maintain the ability to grow in Christ and we will offer an ever more perfect gift of humanity to Our Creator in heaven.

The Eleventh Step Process

STEP #11

Sought through prayer and meditation to improve our conscious contact with God, as we understood Him, praying only for knowledge of His will and the power to carry that out.

SPIRITUAL AWARENESS

BIG BOOK	BIBLE
Spiritual Experience 569-570	Philippians 4: 4- 9
Meditation 86, 88	Psalm 1: 1- 6
	Psalm 91

Whoever clings to me I will deliver;
    whoever knows my name I will set on high.
All who call upon me I will answer;
    I will be with them in distress;
    I will deliver them and give them honor.
With length of days I will satisfy them
    and show them my saving power.
                Psalm 91: 14-16

There are so many things I want to say about this part of the journey. All of the words and feelings and lessons have been written before. Many of us will have deep rooted certainties about prayer and meditation which have held our life together for many years. Now is not the time to change. Now is the time to reflect and deepen and enrich and expand and enhance. *NOW IS THE TIME FOR LOVE IN THE MOST PERSONAL EXPRESSION.*

Rest within the solitude of our heart and soul, fully functioning now with our minds clear and free and filled with the purpose of Our Savior. Be with the Lord in prayer and meditation.

Preparation

It would be normal now to set guidelines and procedures in place. I will only relate some of the tools and ideas that are very helpful to me in this 11th Step process. Please see if these will help you to enhance your spiritual bonding with Christ through prayer and meditation.

Definition of Prayer and Meditation:
☨ Prayer is speaking to God.
☨ Meditation is listening to Him.

Listen to the simplicity of this statement and allow it to fill our imagination. Can we see a Creator who would make this part of the task hard if He wanted us to love Him? Can we imagine a Christ who would give His very life for us but then hide from our striving for personal intimacy?

The first certainty of the 11th Step process is that Jesus Christ has already opened the channel of communications and, if we ask, He will break through and answer us.

If I were to say this just prior to our work effort in the 1st Step we might have laughed and walked away from another hopeless journey. But now, after our own personal involvement with the steps; with our effort and the results already reflected in our lives; we can move to this deeper certainty of Jesus' love.

The second certainty is that our striving must be personal. This is not a time of ritual or formalized worship. This is a time of true and unique communications. This is a dialogue between two real individuals who are in love. There is no more personal experience, at least not known to man.

The third certainty is that God loves us. Our journey through the 12 Steps has proved this beyond a shadow of a doubt. Our journey has given us the personal promises that demonstrate His love for us in so many beautiful ways. Jesus gives His life for us in the greatest sacrifice of love in order to assure our happiness and a way to our Creator's loving arms. There is no more doubt. There is only love, filling our hearts and minds and souls with the peace that comes from a loving God.

Setting Our Personal Goals

I feel nervous in setting goals for anyone at this stage. I am such a child at this part of the journey. Most of my writings have been to understand and enhance this portion of my own program, and to improve my conscious contact with my Lord and Savior. Now I feel unworthy and untrained.

Others will come and fill in the blanks I leave. For now I ask your to accept my musings as from a loving friend on the same path to the Lord's arms.

> All Time Goals:
> 1. Allow your mind to speak freely
> 2. Allow your heart to sing His praise
> 3. Follow the path set by the Holy Spirit
> 4. Keep open the channels He will use
> 5. Tell Him a joke once in a while.

Allow Your Mind to Speak Freely

Prayer is a growing process used throughout our lives. The times of formal prayer are never wasted and remain very important to the whole of our existence. In the 11th Step we are looking at prayer as the deepest form of communication. Here we want to open our minds and speak freely to our God. Here we are in the deepest sense involved in a personal relationship.

This is the first key to enhancement I found. Stumbling through this step was a difficult process. It truly felt funny to speak to God as if I was talking with my wife or a friend.

The need for this relationship was now more powerful than the silly feelings of embarrassment. I knew I wanted to be truly close to my Lord. I knew that this need was real and I could no longer hold back. Sometimes great floods of tears and pain would gush forth. Sometimes great fountains of wonderful joy would burst from me. Mostly, I would want to talk and have someone listen to my little pains and wonderful adventures in life. Once I allowed myself to speak there was no stopping.

I believe this is the culmination of all the previous Steps allowing me the freedom to present my entire humanity to Christ along with the real grace of Our Lord helping me to reach Him and His Love.

Allow Your Heart to Sing His Praise

I am not here, so I must relate the first hand story of one who goes before me and helps me on my journey.

I know a man who has been a gentle guide to my journey with the Lord. In his tenderness, he has tried to show me how to open my heart. I find myself tentative and actually shy. This part of the process is so hard. (I am sure that my wife will be able to confirm this. Through all the puffery and ego, there is a very shy and scared boy inside of me afraid to show my love.)

One night I heard a noise in the other room as I awoke. In the darkness of the early spring morning I arose to find the problem. There in the living room, my friend was deep in prayer with the Lord. In slow and graceful movement he danced with the Lord in the most wonder filled expressions of pleasure and peace. The only word clearly understood by me that morning was ABBA.

I have never been able to be so free with my heart but that morning I could feel the energy and the very presence of the Lord. I almost hated myself for interrupting such a personal moment. I know he did not mind. I know the Lord did not mind. There before me was the reality of meditation of the heart. The opening of oneself to the presence of the Lord. Set your heart free, it was created by God for God!

Follow the Path Set by the Holy Spirit

There are many paths that can be seen within the realm of meditation. I am neither a scholar nor find need to identify them all. This I do know. When we have progressed this far within the spiritual journey of the 12 Steps the Holy Spirit will always guide our steps.

There is no right or wrong. There is relationship. Our Savior will find a way to open the dialogue and fill us with a relationship based on love and understanding.

The Lord's way can be seen most often by the spirit. Maybe this will help:

> I KNOW that Adam and Eve were two individuals who sired the whole world. It says so in the Bible.
>
> I can see the eternal power and the wonderful love of my God in the words of Genesis and the story of Adam and Eve. I can see His eternal love for me!

In both cases there is a profession of faith. One lets the spirit respond to the mysterious wonders of our Creator in heaven.

Set your spirit free!

Keep Open the Channels He Will Use

This sage advice has been given from the beginning of time. It is not a statement of trying all the newest fads in meditation. It is a message of continuance and adaptability.

Most important here is not to lock ourselves into communication with the Lord in private only. We need community. We need to be open to His word in all that we see and read and hear.

In the beginning of this journey we started by using tools of the child so that we could begin with a foundation of safety. Now we need to make sure we do not turn away from that foundation. This was, is, and always will be a "WE PROGRAM." We need to hear the good news from our fellow travelers and we need to strive to learn from them all.

The old timers in the programs have said many times that our growth depends on the newcomers. They know that we will learn more from these young ones than from any of the great ponderings of our now formed minds. It is here that we will find the keys to the changes we need to make.

Once more, no one is an island. We cannot separate ourselves from the Body of Christ.

Tell Him a Joke Once in a While!

In closing this section I offer this test. If in a quiet time with the Lord we cannot tell Him a joke, we are still holding back our love and gifts.

Please use this as a weather vane and realize it is not easy to joke with the Lord. God has always been portrayed with power. The Bible still holds out "The fear of the Lord" for all to see. But truly, can we see the simplicity of this test? Can we feel the reality of this goal? When we laugh together we are already in relationship and very much open and therefore in love.

I hope by this time in the journey we have found a Risen Savior that is filled with the precious gift of laughter.

The Discipline

I want to leave the disciple in your hands. We have already reached the stage of self-discipline. We no longer need constant attention and care. We have felt the power of the Lord in our personal lives and have the keys to keeping this power living within us.

Let me just ask you this one very special favor. Your journey will take you far and give you great insight into your life and your relationship with the Lord in heaven. Be gentle with those who come after you. They will find their way in the time allotted by Christ. Allow them the freedom to grow as I allow you here.

The Twelfth Step Process

STEP #12

Having had a Spiritual Awakening as the result of these Steps, we tried to carry this message to _____, and to practice these principles in all our affairs.

SERVICE

BIG BOOK	BIBLE
Serenity 68, 544, 551, 552	Matthew 22: 36-40
	Philippians 2: 1-18
	Luke 6: 27-36
	II Corinthians 1: 3-11

You have been told, O man, what is good,
and what the Lord requires of you:
Only to do the right and to love goodness,
and to walk humbly with your God.

Micah 6:8

This is the final Step. It is the culmination of a great human and spiritual process.

Our journey has finally come to its *Beginning*.

We are now ready to begin. We have learned many things, we have changed and prepared and mended and even created new parts of our existence. We have received many of the gifts promised by the program. We have the full and wonderful power of Our Loving Savior as part of our lives.

Yes! This is the *Beginning*!

All of this has been done to draw us to this point of beginning. All of our efforts have been in preparation for this moment in our spiritual growth.

Preparation

Listen with our new inner spirit to the words of *"The Prayer of Saint Francis."*

Lord make me a channel of your peace,
that where there is hatred, I may bring love;
that where there is wrong, I may bring the spirit of
      forgiveness;
that where there is error, I may bring truth;
that where there is doubt, I may bring faith;
that where there is despair, I may bring hope;
that where there are shadows, I may bring light;
that where there is sadness, I may bring joy.

Lord, grant that I may seek rather to comfort than to
      be comforted;
to understand than to be understood;
to love than to be loved.

For it is by giving that one receives.
It is by self-forgetting that one finds.
It is by forgiving that one is forgiven.
And it is by dying that one awakens to eternal life.

In this last stanza we see the Key to the 12th Step. Service. Service through Love.

This section has been labeled throughout this book as "Preparation". Truly we are prepared. There is little else to do but to go out and do the will of the Lord.

Setting Our Personal Goals

While each of the previous steps were presented as part of the logical order of this program, they can stand on their own as Christian principles. But listen to the first eleven words of this 12fth Step:

> *Having had a Spiritual Awakening as the result*
> *of these Steps...*

Technically this 12th Step is the process holding within itself the eleven step process we have journeyed through. In the final analysis, it is the fullness of this life itself. It is the great commandment given to us by Jesus.

> *Love one another....*

Our All Time Goals are:

> 1. Remove the Bushel Basket
> 2. Find the Joy
> 3. Watch His Flowers Grow

Remove the Bushel Basket

Jesus said it, preachers everywhere have shouted it from the pulpits and now here we see it again.

Carry the message to _____....

Even before practicing these principles in our own affairs we are entreated to carry the message.

As Christians we have spent too much time hiding within ourselves. When all was darkness and we had nothing to give, we had very little choice. But now it is different and Christ has made it so. Now we are filled with His light. In Matthew 5: 14-16 we see the absurdity of lighting a lamp and putting it under a bushel basket.

We need to reach down into our new-found spirituality and see the absurdity of keeping this "Good News of Jesus Christ" to ourselves.

Now I am the last to say jump up and profess, get out in the public and proclaim. In fact, too many times this has led the giver and receiver of the message astray Listen to the words of the Lord:

> For by the grace given to me I tell everyone among you not to think of himself more highly than one ought to

to the measure of faith that God has appointed. For as in one body we have many parts, and all the parts do not have the same function, so we, though many, are one body in Christ and individually parts of one another. Since we have gifts that differ according to the grace given us, let us exercise them: if prophesy, in proportion to the faith; if ministry, in ministering; if one is a teacher, in teaching; if one exhorts, in exhortation; if one contributes, in generosity; if one is over others, with diligence; if one does acts of mercy, with cheerfulness.

Romans 12: 3-8

We need to allow the grace of Christ to find its way out of our experience to benefit of others.

Maybe this will help:

Like the 10th Step, we are still not the one who controls the environment of the kingdom. Christ will truly and surely lead us to the work He wants done. Furthermore, it is not preaching or teaching but SHARING and CARING that will invite others to the loving arms of Jesus!

It is in our quiet and humble actions of "agape/love" that our light will shine and His work will be accomplished here on earth.

Breathe deeply and think back through the process of these steps. Did He ever ask anything of us that was not to our greater good and benefit? Did He ever give us more than we could handle?

One day at a time, He has filled us with all the grace necessary to do His will and meet our needs. We need to see this and acknowledge it through the acceptance of the SERVICE required in the 12th Step.

Find the Joy

In my DIS-ease, I believed this life was a "purgatory" if not a "hell." Now, in my newly transformed humanity, I see the peace and excitement of His kingdom here on earth.

There has been nothing more lasting and more enjoyable for me than to help another find their way to Christ. I have, (and will proclaim this), found the true joy of Christianity!

At first I believed the joy would be the personal relationship with Jesus built through the first eleven steps; an internal and powerful emotional response to Christ's presence in my spiritual life. This is indeed beautiful beyond expression and very fulfilling but there is a greater reality for me, for us, for humanity.

Teachers have expressed it as "seeing the lights go on."

Priests have witnessed the "feeling of love growing in the community."

I know it as "passing the message on."

Watching the Flowers Grow

If there is one thing that is certain about a spiritual awakening it is that once we've had one we can recognize it in another.

We will never be able to create a spiritual awakening for another person. We will never be able to give ours to another. It truly is an intimate union of one spirit to the eternal heart of Jesus Christ. It has been for us, and will be for everyone else, Christ who will affect this awakening.

So here is the real joy and purpose of this 12th Step. We watch and rejoice in (reliving our own experience) the awakenings of our friends in Christ. Truly there is nothing more spectacular and fulfilling in humanity.

I sit in God's garden of love and tenderly turn the soil. Pulling out the weeds that attack the vines. There in the peace and presence of my Lord, I watch God's flowers grow.

Nothing may ever smell as sweet as a rose, but nothing will ever be as beautiful as the blossoming of the Holy Spirit within a friend.

The Discipline

The discipline is the fulfillment and incorporation of the Twelve Step Process within our lives. To attempt any explanation would be to rewrite the steps and very unnecessary.

We have come a very long way together. And to think, this is just the beginning!

In Closing

I have always loved these words from the Big Book and could not think of a more appropriate message for bringing these writings to a close.

Closing Words from the Big Book:

Abandon yourself to God as you understand God. Admit your faults to Him and to your fellows. Clear away the wreckage of your past. Give freely of what you find and join us. We shall be with you in the Fellowship of the Spirit, and you will surely meet some of us as you trudge the Road of Happy Destiny.

May God bless you and keep you - until then.

Big Book p 164

Thank you for joining me on this journey and I hope that you find the peace and happiness I have found with Jesus Christ in His kingdom here on earth.

I Have A Vision

I have a vision that has filled my heart with joy and wonderful peace.

I really expected it to be different. I expected a more glorious and triumphant show of His power. But instead He came and sat beside me with pains and troubles like those I have felt in my life. I saw His need and I gave what I had.

It was then that my vision was complete. It was then that I truly saw His love. It was then that I finally understood.

I have the vision of the child knowing His father and resting in His arms safe and warm and free. This vision is Jesus Christ.

May you find Him now.

Peace, and may your journey be eventful,

Bill J.

Bibliography

I gratefully acknowledge the following books and articles that served as vital references to this material and my continued personal spiritual growth.

Alberts, Karen. Recover and Heal: Meditations on the Twelve Steps. Cincinnati: St. Anthony Messenger Press, 1992.

Alcoholics Anonymous (the Big Book). New York: Alcoholics Anonymous World Services, Inc., 1976.

Alcoholics Anonymous Comes of Age. New York: Alcoholics Anonymous World Services, Inc., 1983.

Barkley, Roy. The Catholic Alcoholic. Huntington, IN: Our Suinday Visitor, Inc., 1990.

Grateful Members. The Twelve Steps for Everyone...Who Wants Them. Minneapolis: Compcare Publishers, 1975.

Gustin, Marilyn Norquist. The Inward Journey (Discovering Your Spiritual Self). Ligouri, MO: Ligouri Publications, 1991.

Living Recovery: Inspirational Moments for Twelve Step Living. New York: Ballantine Books, 1990.

McMakin, Jacqueline, with Rhoda Nary. Doorways to Christian Growth. San Francisco: Harper, 1984.

Miller, Kieth. A Hunger for Healing: The Twelve Steps as a Classic Model for Christian Spiritual Growth. San Francisco: Harper, 1991.

_____. A Taste of New Wine. San Francisco: Harper, 1973.

Powell, John, S.J. Unconditional Love. Allen, TX: Argus Communications.

Rohr, Richard, O.F.M. Breathing Under Water - Spirituality of the Twelve Steps. Catholic Update, Sept. 1990. N. pag.

_____. The Twelve Steps: An Amazing Gift of the Spirit. n.p., n.d.

Saint Joseph Edition of the New American Bible (the Big, Big Book). New York: Catholic Book Publishing Co., 1992.

St. Romain, Philip. Twelve Steps to Spiritual Wholeness. Ligouri, MO: Ligouri Publications, 1992.

Twenty-Four Hours a Day. n.p., Hazelden Foundation, 1975.

A MESSAGE FROM BILL J. AND
VISION MANAGEMENT

You have purchased a book with a history. Its past goes back 2000 years and beyond to include even our Jewish traditions of seeking the Lord. I hope that you have found something here that has given both **HOPE** for your personal journey and **JOY** in the process of being in love with the Lord. If so, then the present history of this book is complete. It has told one more individual how much Jesus Christ really loves them.

I would like you to take a moment and to think with me about the future history of this book. It should be placed on a convenient shelf where it can be used again and again. But maybe it needs to be passed on. Maybe you know of someone who should hear this message of the Lord. In that case, I ask you to pray with all of us at Vision Management and seek your way of providing this work to others.

Additional copies of this book can be purchased by writing or calling:

Vision Management
5202 Fox Trail Lane
Colleyville, TX 76034
(817) 355-1816

Here are the discounts available for you and those you know who would enjoy this journey with the Lord:

Number of Books	Unit Price Per Book	
1	$10.95	Please add $3.00 for shipping and handling. Texas residents please include sales tax (8.75%)
2-24	9.85	
25-99	9.30	The workbook, *The Care and Feeding of the Mustard Seed And Other Traditions of God's Love for Us*, is also available for $12.45.
100-499	7.10	
500-999	5.45	
1000+	CALL	

OTHER 12 STEP MATERIALS FROM VISION MANAGEMENT

The Walk with the Lord Seminar
Designed as a 4 session 8 hour introduction to the principles and the Christian traditions process of the 12 Steps. This seminar is very effective in starting a 12 Step Group within your church community. Vision Management can provide the speakers and material to make this seminar a real beginning for many in your church. By covering expenses, Vision Management will lead your core group through the details and present this program. A love donation for the continuing mission of the 12 Steps to Spirituality would be appropriate.

The Journey of Love and Service Retreat
A weekend of love and deep meditation with the Lord. This retreat is focused on celebrating the ongoing process of the 12 Steps and to revitalize those on the journey. It is tremendously effective when your 12 Step church group reaches 8 to 12 months of maturity and helps to refocus the efforts of those involved. Again, by covering expenses, Vision Management will lead your core group through the details and present this program. A love donation for the continuing mission of the 12 Steps to Spirituality would be appropriate.

OTHER 12 STEP MATERIALS FROM VISION MANAGEMENT

The Care and Feeding of the Mustard Seed
And Other Traditions of God's Love for Us
This is a workbook that looks at the HOW TOs for the 12 Step program and helps the user to journal and follow the pathway. Each chapter presents questions to explore as you come to understand the work the Lord has for you in this process and provides information and experiential items to solidify your understanding of the 12 Steps. Written in coordination with the 12 Steps to Spirituality Group, it remains in binder form so that it can grow and enhance the lives of those who journey through the Steps.

Step by Step for the Christian Group's Development
This pamphlet provides thoughts, action plans and advice on how to start and nurture a 12 Step Group in your own church community. Please call Vision Management and they will be glad to deliver one copy to you at no charge.

A VISION OF LOVE AND SERVICE

The journey begins with an internal urging to be something more and do something with this life we have been given. Step by Step we find the peace and serenity that God has always wanted for us. If this has been your experience, then please read on and pray with us at Vision Management.

The Vision Management team is dedicated to the continuation of small Christian Communities that live and share this process of 12 Step Spirituality. Working with church groups and other organizations we foster communication between groups and help people begin 12 Step Groups of their own.

While each group should remain autonomous, we need to be in community. So here is the straight forward pitch:

1. Please pray for groups that are taking on the challenge of forming Christian Communities based upon the 12 Step Traditions of Love and Service to the Lord. Your prayers will help most of all. If you also feel a calling to start a group for yourself and your community, contact us. We will be glad to help however we can.

2. If you can, please think about a love donation for this cause. Each dollar helps us to spread the work we have begun with these books, the retreats and seminars available. It is simple work and your prayers will discern for you if it is worthy work for the Lord's vineyard.

Thank you and God bless,

The Vision Management Team
5202 Fox Trail Lane
Colleyville, TX 76034
(817) 355-1816